TRUTHS THAT SET YOU FREE

"If you continue in my word,
you are truly my disciples
and you will know The Truth,
and The Truth will set you free."
Jesus The Messiah
JOHN 8:31–32

TOM MURRAY
founder of Truth Seekers Fellowship

ISBN-13: 978-1491240458

ISBN-10: 1491240458

©2013 Truth Seekers Fellowship
First Edition 2013, CreateSpace

For Jeannie

Vision: It is the responsibility of the Body of Christ (The Church) as a whole to "make disciples of all nations" (Matthew 28:18) and grow them to spiritual maturity in Christ. Truth Seekers Fellowship assists the Body of Christ in the primary ministry sphere of Teaching by offering Christ focused, Biblical instruction and by training and equipping others in the teaching ministry. All of this is done with a view to promoting Oneness in the Body of Christ (John 17:20-21, Ephesians 4:1-6).

What? We **Proclaim Christ** by **warning** all people and **teaching** all people with all wisdom so that we may **present** every person mature in Christ. Toward this goal **we labor**, struggling according to His power that powerfully works in us. (Colossians 1:28-29)

How? Truth Seekers Fellowship exists to:
1. **Create** Christ-focused, Bible Based curriculum that promotes Life Transformation, not merely information transfer.
2. **Develop** classes, resources and tools around our Milk to Meat strategy of teaching the core elements of the faith with a view to cultivating mature disciples of Christ.
3. **Invest** in the lives of willing and hungry students in both the "classroom" setting, but even more importantly in smaller "life on life" contexts.

Connect: www.tsfmemphis.org
connect@tsfmemphis.org
(901) 685-3385

Contents

Foreword

"We are only here a short time ... Maximize your journey."

These are the words of Tom Murray, a beloved friend and extraordinary teacher, who went to be with his Lord on August 26, 2005. Tom was one of those *Reader's Digest* "Most Unforgettable Characters." Once introduced, you really could never get him out of your mind, nor did you want to. He had a depth and breadth of knowledge of God's Word only a few people can claim, especially lay folks.

It really wasn't his photographic memory that wooed you; it was his understanding of the Gospel and his ability to "make it real" in *your* life. Few could envision like Tom. Few could organize like Tom. Few could attract people like Tom. And nobody could teach like Tom. He was well equipped. No one ever had to guess what Tom's greatest gifts were; it was his teaching and his ability to connect with people out of his love for Christ.

Tom was into multiplication—he wanted to make disciples and have those disciples make other disciples and then have those disciples make even more disciples. He knew how the math worked: Tom *multiplied* in one discipleship class of 20 *multiplied* by those 20 teaching 20 others *equals* 400 and so on. He was just doing what Jesus did which is always a pretty good example to follow!

I remember when God called Tom from Holiday Paint & Drywall to the mission field. Now, how many people do you know in mid-life who completely close down a business and follow God's calling? You for sure have to be faithful; you have to be listening; you have to be obedient and you have to follow His lead and act. I suppose Tom had a connection to Christ that many of us don't have—it was like a "direct line." He was absolutely positive this is what God had prepared him for all his life. What a blessing to realize and understand this then to go out and live it.

In my Bible today, I have green magic maker throughout highlighting every "In Christ," "In Jesus," "In Him," "Through Christ," "Through Jesus," "Through Him," etc. Tom taught me this and he encouraged me to remember that whenever we see these "In Christ" statements they should heighten our attention. One of my favorite sound bites from Tom is, "God always initiates and we always respond." I have thought about that phrase many times over the years.

I am so grateful for the materials I have from Tom, for the lessons he taught, for the tapes he made, for the radio ministry he had. I cherish the MilktoMeat classes, the countless Emmaus and Chrysalis Walks we had together, an unbelievable trip to Israel, the many social gatherings we found ourselves at and the few private consultations I had with him. *His touch was powerful; he left his fingerprints everywhere.*

I have always said that the three most important aspects of life are faith, family and friends and boy, did Tom have them ALL! He had an unmatched faith in Christ and complete assurance of his position. He had a wife and family he absolutely adored and was sooooo proud of. And he had more friends than one can imagine. He made a tremendous impact on every person he came in contact with.

It occurred to me that time is short and we all need to enlarge, increase and intensify our own journey. Tom Murray should be the glowing example to all of us. To hear Tom give his own funeral benediction through his recordings was both emotionally moving and personally inspiring; he was teaching us right up to the end.

In His Steps,
C. Kemmons Wilson, Jr.

Preface

In 1993, Tom Murray sold his business and followed the Lord into full-time, vocational ministry. Truth Seekers Fellowship was born out of Tom's vision and exhortation: *"Make your journey worthy of your destination."* Pursuing this goal, Tom practiced his gift of teaching with insight, wisdom and a dry wit that resonated with his students in a truly unique way: *focusing them on Christ, grounding them in His Word.*

One of Tom's first studies for Truth Seekers Fellowship was entitled "Truths That Set You Free." To celebrate the 20th Anniversary of the founding of the ministry, that first study has been shaped into the book you hold now. This study was the "seed" which sprouted into our larger Milk*to*Meat curriculum and it represents the foundation of our ministry. It is a major part of Tom's legacy that lives on in the ministry of Truth Seekers Fellowship. As the writer of Hebrews says, " … *and through faith, though he is dead, he still speaks"* (Hebrews 11:4).

I think if we could speak to Tom now, he would remind us of what he used to teach: "Anyone *in Christ* never really dies; he just 'graduates' into the Lord's presence." Tom has been in the Lord's presence for almost eight years now; I would love to hear what he could teach us now.

Our hope and prayer is that as you read this book, you will get a little taste of Tom's humor and a big dose of his wisdom. Above all, we hope that you will develop an appetite for the Truth that will set you free in Christ.

Stacy Tyson
General Director
Truth Seekers Fellowship
2013

CHAPTER 1

Dead in Adam or Alive in Christ

*"In Adam all Die,
but in Christ all will be made alive."*
1 CORINTHIANS 15:22

I n October of 1967 I was 26 years old and I was biblically illiterate. I didn't know John 3:16 and couldn't have found it if you had handed me a Bible. I had people who tried to talk to me about Christianity and get me to church, but I never really understood any of it. I wasn't hostile—it just never made sense. Christianity was presented to me as a set of rules, rituals, sacraments—things you did or people you hung around with.

To be honest, I looked at Christians as a narrow bunch of people that I had no desire to be around. I thought, "These people are afraid to die and they don't know how to live." Coming from a public housing project, playing football to get into college, I wasn't afraid to die and I certainly wasn't afraid to live. At that point, I had no desire to be a Christian because I had met some!

But then some of those Christians asked me, "Why do think God made a man in the first place? How did God design that man to function? What do you think went wrong? and What do you think

God did to fix the mess?" Those were the questions that changed everything for me.

We are going to start by dealing with those four basic questions. In answering those questions we will get to the bottom of the Gospel. It wasn't until I understood the answers to those questions that the Gospel made sense to me. As we work with these questions, we are also going to talk about the difference between being "Dead in Adam" as opposed to being "Alive in Christ."

Why Did God Create a Man?

In Genesis 1:26 God says, "Let us make mankind in our image." What does this mean? The short answer is God is saying, "Let's engineer a man in such a way that when all the world looks at him, they can see what I'm like."

Well what is God like? There are many different ways we could answer that question, but we are going to focus on one of the most important. You have probably heard the saying, "God is love." That statement comes from the Bible in 1 John 4:8 and 16. We are going to make the case that when God created the first man, he did so to display this central part of his character: *love*. When God created a man, he did so in order that all mankind could experience God's love and then reflect God's love.

The Three Types of Love

To really understand God's love, we need to talk about some other types of love. The first kind of "love" we are going to call Candy "love." Candy "love" is the kind of love where I say to a child, "If you'll hug my neck, I'll give you a piece of candy." This type of "love" is based on reward; it's a bribe. You give me something that I want, and I'll give you something that you want.

The opposite of that type of "love" is what we'll call Smack "love". An example of this type of "love" is if I say to a child, "If you don't love me, I'm gonna smack you." This is a type of "love" that is motivated out of threat and fear. This is an ugly, false "love" that too often leads to abuse.

Then there is real love—Genuine Love. That's the kind of love that comes with no strings attached. It's like when my wife comes and sits in my lap when I'm in the midst of reading a book or doing something. All of sudden, she's there in my lap. She's been doing that for 27 years now.

The first thing I say to her is, "What have you done?"

She says, "I haven't done anything!"

Next question: "What do you want me to do?"

She says, "I don't want you to do anything."

"Then what are you doing in my lap!? You've either done something, or you want something, that's the only reason anybody climbs in anybody's lap."

But she says, "I'm here because I just want to love you." That's real love. It's not candy. It's not smack. It's real.

Well, if God is love, which of those kinds of love do you think God is? He is the real thing. Now some people try to bribe men and women with, "God loves you and He's got a heck of a deal. If you'll love Him, He'll forgive all your sins and then, when you die, he'll take you to heaven. In the meantime, he won't make any demands. He'll stay off your back and you can run your life and do as you please and ignore him." What kind of love is that? That's candy. And when the candy runs out, they will question God's love.

There are others you who say, "If you don't love God, you'll fry brother; He's gonna burn you in Hell." Now you can scare the hell out of people with that type of smack "love." You can get them to raise their hand and run down an aisle. They'll come up and get sprinkled or dunked in your church, but it may not be real. You probably just scared them. Six months later, you might wonder where they have gone.

But then there's the real love. That's the genuine love of God. That's the kind He loves us with. That is the kind of love we hear about in John 3:16, "For God so loved the world that He gave His only Son ..." That is the kind of love He has created us to experience and reflect.

How Did God Design the Man to Function?

So when God created the first man Adam, he created him in such a way to produce his image. Take a look at the following diagram. We are going to try to illustrate the parts that made up Adam when He was created:

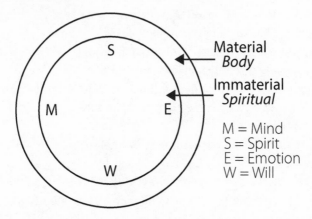

Adam would have had a body. This "outside" part of Adam is what we will call his "material part." On the "inside" Adam had personality like God; he had a **M**ind, **E**motion and **W**ill. That's what God gave to Adam because it requires mind, emotion and will to be a person. Those are also necessary to have a relationship with God because He has those too. He also put within Adam a human **S**pirit. We will call all those parts his "immaterial parts."

Now remember, God said, "Let us make a man in our image." Well if man was made in God's image, then when God looked at the man He saw himself. That's why when He completed the creation He said, "It is very good" (Genesis 1:31). In the beginning, the man was made to be the image of God in Creation and that is what he was.

Two Types of Image

Now, we need to talk very briefly about two kinds of image. The first type of image is an *image by imitation*. Imagine if I were an artist and I got Jim to come and sit for me as I painted a portrait. After several sittings I told Jim, "Look, it's not necessary anymore for you to come, I'm gonna do all the finishing touches and I'll let you know when I have the finished product." So Jim gets up and leaves.

Now imagine Jim's wife comes in right behind him, looks at my painting and says, "It looks just like him!" I would say, "Yes" as I begin to swell up with pride, "What do you expect?" She says, "Has Jim seen this?" I say, "Well no, he just went out the door."

Now imagine her rushing out the door, grabbing Jim and congratulating him: "That is some painting! Its great!"

As the artist who painted the painting, I'm getting a little mad and I come out in the hall and say, "Don't congratulate him; He was like a bump on a log. He didn't do anything. If there's anybody to be congratulated it's me!" If the image on the canvas bears any resemblance to the original, you don't congratulate the person in the picture, you congratulate the artist who painted the picture. It was my painting, my talent, my brushes. I did it. Now that's an image by imitation.

Now there is a second kind of image and it is *a derived or reflected image.* That's the image you get when you look in the mirror. All a mirror does is give you back what you give it. It was created that way. If you'd like to know whether or not God has a sense of humor, before you shower in the morning, just look in the mirror. I crack up every morning. God has a terrific sense of humor!

The image in the mirror is derived from your presence; it is reflected. If you leave, the image leaves as well. But the imitation image on the canvas stays because it is just an imitation. So the question becomes when God said "let us make a man in our image," was His image imparted by imitation or did God intend for man to reflect Him, like a mirror?

In this case, it is best to understand that God intended for mankind to *reflect* His image. *This would require God's presence in order for man to reflect the image of God.* Man was not just imitating the image of God as in a painting; he would derive his image from the presence of God.

Now in our diagram, we will draw in a little triangle with an L in it which will represent Life. This will represent Adam's ability to reflect the presence of God and share His life.

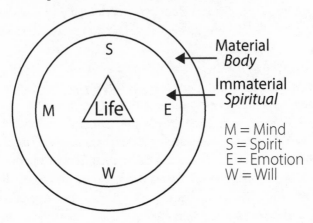

So you see as Adam lived in the presence of God, God's image would reflect in his mind, his emotion and his will and the life of God would govern his behavior. In this way, when you watched Adam behave, you were actually seeing God behave. That's how he was to reflect the image of God, like a mirror, but you never congratulate a mirror. If you had happened to be there when Adams was first created, you would see what God was like clothed in humanity. You wouldn't have congratulated Adam. He would have said, "Don't congratulate me; without God's presence within me, I would not be able to reflect His image."

What Went Wrong?

Now, when Adam was created, he was created righteous which means everything was good, everything was right, everything worked as it was supposed to. This "created righteousness" manifested itself as innocence, but his innocence needed to be tested. There had to be a test to see if man, given the option, would chose to love God.

You see along with the capacity to love, there must be the ability to chose. In fact, it was Adam's ability to say "no" to God that would make his "yes" so meaningful. Had God not given Adam the ability to say "no" to Him, Adam would have been a robot. When Adam behaved, he wouldn't be saying anything to God. He wouldn't have any option.

So God gave man an option. He gave Adam the ability to choose to say "no." We are going to call this ability *the power of contrary choice*. It is the ability to choose to do something that is outside the wisdom and instruction of God.

Adam's test came in the form of the one negative command that God gave him: "You shall not eat from the tree of the knowledge of Good and Evil for on the day you eat of it you will absolutely die" (Genesis 2:17). Now for a while, Adam walked with God, he knew God. He enjoyed that relationship with God but you know the story. There came a time when Adam exercised his option and ate from the forbidden tree. It was as if he was saying to God, "I don't want this relationship. I want to be free from you." God had determined to let Adam reap the consequences of his choice and there were two consequences to this choice.

The first consequence was that Adam died spiritually. Now, God had clearly told Adam, "In the day that you eat of that tree you will surely die." But the day Adam made that choice, he didn't die physically. He lived for 930 years before his physical death came. However, on that day he did die spiritually. When Adam exercised his power of contrary choice, the life of God which was derived from the presence of God, was taken from Adam.

The second consequence came in the form of Adam not being able to reflect the image of God perfectly anymore. After his rebellion, if you looked at Adam, he didn't reflect the image of God clearly as was intended. You could say that Adam's mirror was cracked or that it was marred.

Adam had failed his test and his failure not only affected him, it affected us all. Now as Adam and Eve began to have children they couldn't give to them what they no longer had—the life of God and the ability to reflect God's image perfectly. Every boy and girl born into this world after Adam's rebellion has been born physically alive but spiritually dead because Adam could not give to his heirs what he didn't have. So now our circles would look something like this:

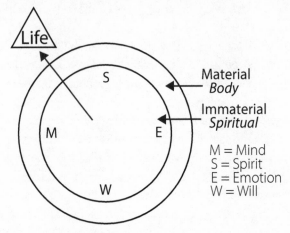

When you look at people today who are not Christians, you don't see them reflecting the goodness of God fully as was intended. This is why there's rape and murder and adultery. Think about this: Have you ever seen an alcoholic horse? No horse would be that stupid. It takes a man to do that. Have you ever seen a cat blow his mind on drugs? No cat would be that stupid. It takes a person to do that—a person who is not governed by God and can't control themselves. We are clever enough to put a man on the moon but the minute we build a satellite, we arm it with nuclear weapons and point it back at the earth. Does that make any sense?

It is incredible what a man can do, but left to himself, he can't manage himself. This is because God never intended for man to manage himself. God intended that mankind would be content in a love relationship with him so that God could live with us and we would reflect His goodness in all that we are and do.

But after Adam's "no," mankind is now in a terrible dilemma. If left on their own, Adam and Eve and their descendants (all of us) would be lost forever. However, God did something. He intervened so that we would have another option, another chance to say "yes" to God instead of just dying under the terrible consequences of Adam's "no." This way of escape that God provided is the good news of the Gospel.

What Did God Do?

Why have we spent so much time talking about Adam in the Garden of Eden? It is because you cannot understand what happened at the Cross unless you understand what happened in the Garden of Eden. And you cannot fully understand what happened in the Garden of Eden unless you understand what happened at the Cross. What Christ was doing at the cross was correcting what happened with Adam in the Garden of Eden.

In order to provide another option for our terrible dilemma, God sent his Son—the Lord Jesus Christ—to this earth with a body just like yours and mine and with personality just like us. But there was something very different about Jesus.

You see, an amazing thing was possible because Jesus was not born of a man. He was conceived in the womb of the virgin Mary by the power of the Holy Spirit:

> "And the angel answered Mary, "The Holy Spirit will come upon you, and the power of the Most High will overshadow you; therefore the child to be born will be called holy—the Son of God. (Luke 1:35)

Jesus was born in the same condition that Adam was created — He was righteous. Since He was not one of Adam's descendants, He did not inherit any of the terrible consequences of Adam's sin. That's why the Bible calls Him "the last Adam" (1 Corinthians 15:45). For the first time since Adam fell, there was a man on the earth that was normal—what God intended in creating a man. That's why the virgin birth of Jesus Christ isn't up for debate. If Jesus Christ had an earthly father, He too would have been be born "Dead in Adam" and He couldn't be the Savior because He would also need a savior.

When we look at the life of the Lord Jesus, it is clear that He lived in fellowship with God and never once said "no." Over the thirty something years of His life, Jesus never exercised the power of contrary choice; He always said "yes" to his Heavenly Father. His own testimony was, "I always do those things that please my father" (John 8:29).

When Philip asked Jesus "Lord shows us the Father," Jesus said "Philip, have you been with me this long and you haven't understood? If you have seen me, you have seen the Father" (John 14:8-9). Jesus didn't say to Philip, "Come here about 10:00 in the morning and I'll strike a pose." He wouldn't have done that. Instead all anyone has to do is look at Jesus twenty-four hours a day, seven days a week, 365 days a year—if you see Jesus, you see the Father.

When Jesus eats breakfast in the morning, you see the Father. When Jesus does laundry, you see the Father. When Jesus is walking down the road, long before He ever preached, you see the Father. Twenty-four hours a day, Jesus lived in such a relationship with the Heavenly Father that He allowed Him access to all that He was so that all the world can look at Jesus and see what God is like. That's why all of the world looked at Him and said "You are not like us!"

Jesus Came to Give Us Life

In John 10:10 Jesus says, "I have come that you might have life and have it abundantly." Think about this: Who needs life? Dead people need life! Those who heard Jesus speak these words weren't physically dead but they were spiritually dead. We could paraphrase what Jesus was saying as, "I've come so that you might have what Adam lost: spiritual life."

In order to understand how Jesus is able to give us Life, we need to understand what happened to Jesus on the Cross. Jesus was on the cross from about 9:00 in the morning until 3:00 in the afternoon. From 9 until noon, he suffered the wrath of men. They spit on him, they reviled him, they accused him, they mocked him, and they chided him. It was during this time that Jesus prayed, "Father forgive them, they don't know what they are doing" (Luke 23:34).

Then about noon, Luke tells us that a great darkness came over the face of the whole earth. Not just the Middle East and not just Golgotha, but over the whole earth, because from noon until three, Jesus would suffer the wrath of God. As Paul says, "He who knew no sin became sin for us" (2 Corinthians 5:21). At noon, Jesus took our place, He became an offering for our sins.

What would have to happen in order for Jesus to become the sacrifice for our sins? He had to face death in all of its forms—both physical and spiritual. You can think of the darkness that began at noon as signifying Jesus' spiritual death. The first consequence of Adam's fall was that he died spiritually—he was cut off from the life of God.

In the great darkness that came upon Jesus at noon, He too was cut off from the Life of the Father. He enters into that condition in which you and I were born. During that time Jesus cried out, "My God, My God why have you forsaken me?" (Matthew 27:46; Psalm 22:1) Have you ever wondered why He said that? This is the only time in the Bible where Jesus addresses God as anything other than Father. In those three hours, He wasn't in a paternal relationship, He was in a *judicial relationship*. For those three hours, He became sin, a sin offering for us. He took our sins on Himself just as the Prophet Isaiah had foretold many years before:

> "Surely He has borne our griefs
>   and carried our sorrows;
> Yet we esteemed Him stricken,
>   smitten by God, and afflicted.
> But He was pierced for our transgressions;
>   He was crushed for our iniquities;
> Upon him was the chastisement that brought us peace,
>   and with His wounds we are healed." Isaiah 53:4–5

The writer of Hebrews also tells us,

> "Jesus offered up prayers and supplications, with loud cries and tears, to Him who was able to save Him from death, and He was heard because of His reverence." Hebrews 5:7

Now, we know that Jesus' cry for help was answered. In His suffering on the Cross, Jesus satisfied the justice of God so that mankind could now be fully restored in relationship to God. At the end of those three hours, Jesus knew that He had accomplished this work and so He said, "*It is finished*" (John 19:30). Notice He doesn't say, "*I* am finished," He says, "*It* is finished." Jesus had completed the work the Father had given Him to do.

Now the darkness lifted. You could think of that darkness representing spiritual death, being cut off from the Life of God. One of the last things Jesus says on the Cross is "Father into your hands I commit my spirit" (Luke 23:46) Notice, Jesus didn't say "God" He said "Father." Jesus was through with His sacrificial work —taking our sins on Himself as a sin offering. He was now back in relationship with God as His Father. He had accomplished His mission and He was going back to the Father.

At this point they took Jesus' body off the Cross and placed it in a grave. His spirit had gone to the Father, His body went to the grave—that is physical death. As we said, Jesus experiences death in all of its forms for us. But then, on the third day Jesus rose physically from the grave.

Jesus' life was restored completely in both its forms, spiritual and physical. Just as the consequence of Adam's sin had been death in all its forms, the consequence of Jesus' righteous life was life in all its forms. That is why Jesus can say, "I have come that you may have life and have it abundantly!" (John 10:10).

You know the rest of the story. About forty days later, Jesus went back up into heaven to the Father in His resurrected body. He had accomplished His mission. Right now, as you read this book, He is seated at the right hand of the Father because He has accomplished all that we needed to be set right with God, to regain all that Adam lost.

How Will You Respond?

So back in October of 1967 when I was 26 years old, I promise you if you had seen me, you wouldn't have seen God. If anybody had come saying, "I think I'd like to see God, let's go look at Tom Murray," you would not have seen God! As I said, I was completely biblically illiterate, I didn't know Jesus, and I didn't understand the Gospel.

I was in a church meeting back on that night in October and I'd been thinking about these questions for a while. That night I knew one thing for sure: I knew that I didn't have Christ. Once I understood that, I learned that the Bible promised that anyone born spiritually "dead in Adam" who wanted to love God back—not out of candy, not out of smack—had been given an option in Christ.

Jesus made a way for those of us that wanted to say "Yes" to God where Adam had said "No." Now that was good news. So, I said, "Lord, I want to make that trade." That night I became a Christian.

That night a lot of people decided to receive Christ. As it turned out there were some counselors that were helping everybody and they ran out of counselors so nobody could help me. Now after I have had time to think about that, I am glad because nobody confused me. At that point I knew just enough. I went all by myself in the corner of our auditorium and I prayed a prayer that you would laugh at. I was a child, a sinner, immature. I just simply said to God, "I never understood, but I do now and I want to trade. If you love me enough to go to the cross, I want you to know that I love you enough to let you come in. I would like to see what you can do with my life; restore your image in me." I'll bet at that moment the Lord Jesus turned to his Father and said, "There's one of those characters; He actually admits that he is spiritually dead and that he wants to love us back. Now Father he doesn't deserve life on his own merit but for my sake, forgive him—For my sake."

That night, in the corner of our church in a little pew, the Holy Spirit came to inhabit my human spirit. Paul tells us in Romans 8:16 that, "the Holy Spirit himself bears witness with our spirit that we are the children of God." There were no bells, no whistles, no horns, no angels sang in my ear, no flash of lightning. He just gave me back what Adam lost—Life. I had been Dead in Adam, but now I was born again; I was Alive in Christ.

Now lets take a look at our diagram one more time—this is what everyone "Alive In Christ" looks like:

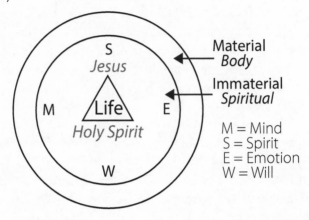

Our text simply says this: "In Adam, all die but in Christ all shall be made alive" (1 Corinthians 15:22). When God looks upon the world today, He sees those that are still Dead in Adam or He sees those who are Alive in Christ. We are all in one of those two positions. We are born Dead in Adam but we have the option to trust Christ, receive Him, receive His life. That's the Gospel. That's the good news. The minute the life of God is restored to the soul of any person, the likeness of God can be restored to the character of that person.

What is Eternal Life?

In John 3:16 God tells us that whoever believes in Jesus has eternal life. Now eternal life is not a feeling you get inside and it is not really a place that you are going to go when you die. Eternal life doesn't even begin when you die. Eternal life is a person. Jesus said "I am The Way, I am The Truth and I am The Life (John 14:6). John wants to make this issue clear for us in his writings:

"And this is the testimony, that God gave us eternal life, and this life is IN his Son. Whoever has the Son has life; whoever

does not have the Son of God does not have life."
(1 John 5:11-12)

John wrote that about fifty years after Christ had gone back to the Father. John is an old man. He's had many years in the field of ministry. Late in his life, he wants to make sure the record is straight, He wants to make sure everyone understands that *Jesus is life*; if you have Jesus you have eternal life. If you don't have Jesus you don't have life. It is just that simple.

If we have Christ we have what he is—LIFE. And we receive that Life the very moment He comes to live within us.

You don't have to be a professional theologian to understand that. I can hand that to almost any child and say, "What does that mean?" In those verses John speaks clearly without all the veneer, without any of the creeds and doctrinal confessions and he says that the bottom line in the Christian life is Christ plus NOTHING.

So why did God create a man? Because he wanted that man to experience His love and be able to love. How did He equip the man to function? He gave him personality and life. What went wrong? Man said "no." What did God do to make it right? He sent Jesus Christ who became our sin offering, took the penalty of our sin upon Himself so that we can say "yes" and step out of death and back into life. That's The Good News.

Now you have heard the good news. Now you have heard God's offer in Christ. *How will you respond*?

Prayer
Father, we thank you for your truth that sets us free from being Dead in Adam. I thank you that you have been so kind to come and make a way of escape for all of us. I understand that we are all are born Dead in Adam but we don't have to stay there. We have the fantastic option of just admitting that we are Dead and that we would like to have new Life in Christ. So we pray that we'll understand that truth and build upon it so that we will discover the fantastic enjoyment that You have in mind as You invite us to live as Your children. We pray that in Christ's name. Amen.

CHAPTER 2

Your Position vs. Your Condition

*So then, if anyone is in Christ, he is a new creation; what is old has
passed away–now look, what is new has come!*
2 CORINTHIANS 5:17

I f you had seen Prince Charles of England the day he was born,
he looked like every other baby. All he could really do was let
people know when he was wet, when he was miserable, when
he was hungry. If you had only seen him lying in his cradle you
probably would not have know that he was His Royal Highness,
Prince Charles Philip Arthur George, Prince of Wales and Earl of
Chester, Duke of Cornwall, Duke of Rothesay, Earl of Carrick, Baron
of Renfrew, Lord of the Isles, Prince and Great Steward of Scotland.
Despite all the names, he looked like every other five minute old
baby. Yet the very moment he was born into that household, he
inherited billions. How much did he know about that? Nothing.
He just wanted a bottle! While he was incredibly wealthy, he was
still just an infant.

The minute you became a child of God, you too became
incredibly wealthy. This is true not only when you get to heaven, it
is true right now. In the Scriptures, our Heavenly Father has revealed
the birthrights and blessings that came to us the very moment of

our spiritual re-birth. They're found primarily in the letters of the New Testament, especially those of Paul. As you read these letters, you might want to underline or highlight every time Paul uses the little prepositional phrase "in Christ" or "in Him" or "in Whom." Usually that will be attached to a blessing that is yours because you are a child of God, IN Christ. Take a few minutes to read through some of these:

"(We) are justified by his grace as a gift, through the redemption that is in Christ Jesus … " (Romans 3:24)

"So you also must consider yourselves dead to sin and alive to God in Christ Jesus." (Romans 6:11)

"For the wages of sin is death, but the free gift of God is eternal life in Christ Jesus our Lord." (Romans 6:23)

"… to those sanctified in Christ Jesus, called to be saints together with all those who in every place call upon the name of our Lord Jesus Christ, both their Lord and ours … " (1 Corinthians 1:2)

"Therefore, if anyone is in Christ, he is a new creation. The old has passed away; behold, the new has come." (2 Corinthians 5:17)

"… for in Christ Jesus you are all sons of God, through faith." (Galatians 3:26)

"Blessed be the God and Father of our Lord Jesus Christ, who has blessed us in Christ with every spiritual blessing in the heavenly places, …" (Ephesians 1:3–4)

"But now in Christ Jesus you who once were far off have been brought near by the blood of Christ." (Ephesians 2:13)

"In Him we have boldness and access with confidence to God through our faith in him." (Ephesians 3:12)

> "He has delivered us from the domain of darkness and
> transferred us to the kingdom of his beloved Son, in whom
> [Christ] we have redemption, the forgiveness of sins."
> (Colossians 1:13–14)

At that very moment you trust Christ, a radical transformation takes place. It's the amazing kind of transformation you see when a caterpillar becomes a butterfly. Paul says, "If anyone is in Christ, he is a new creation. The old has passed away; Look! the new has come!" (Corinthians 5:17 NET).

A caterpillar goes into the cocoon and that same caterpillar goes through a radical change and comes out the other side as a butterfly. It's the same caterpillar, but a miracle takes place. A butterfly can do a lot of things that a caterpillar can't. Caterpillars can't fly; butterflies can. So it is for everyone who is transformed in Christ; a new creation has come, the old has passed away.

Position vs. Condition

> "… those He called He justified, those He justified He also
> glorified."(Romans 8:30)

The minute you become a child of God you cease to be "IN Adam"—spiritually dead and enslaved to sin—and you are placed "IN Christ"—spiritually alive, justified, sanctified, glorified. *Your position has changed.* The very moment we trust Christ, we are Justified—set in right relationship with God—and also *positionally glorified.* As far as God is concerned, In Christ you are now seated in the heavenly realms with Christ:

> "Even when we were dead in our trespasses, God made us
> alive together with Christ—by grace you have been saved—
> and raised us up with Him and seated us with Him in the
> heavenly places in Christ Jesus, so that in the coming ages he
> might show the immeasurable riches of his grace in kindness
> toward us in Christ Jesus." (Ephesians 2:5–7)

This is what we call *positional glorification*. It doesn't look like you and I are seated in the Heavenly realms in Christ, but we are talking about spiritual truth. *This is spiritually, positionally true of everyone IN Christ right now!* Not many of us who are In Christ on earth look very glorious. But from God's point of view, that is who we are—glorified in Christ. Even though we are technically not glorified yet (we don't have our new, glorified bodies) it is as good as done because God will be faithful to finish what He starts with everyone who is In Christ.

One day, I will trade this body I have now for my eternal body, and then I will be glorified completely, made perfect. That will be true of you if you are In Christ. In the meantime, we're gonna have a mean time. That's normality. But God has given you all your birthrights to equip you for what lies ahead. He's given you everything you need to get to the finish line. He has not made you sinless, yet, but he has given you everything you need to "run the race" that is before you, to win every spiritual battle you will face.

One of the great birthright blessings that came to you is that the Holy Spirit baptized you into The Body of Christ and also came to live within you (see Romans 8:9-11, 13:12; 1 Corinthians 3:16).

It is amazing to realize that the Holy Spirit lives in all of us who are In Christ. As the Holy Spirit comes to live within us, the presence of Christ dwells within us as well:

> I pray that according to the wealth of His glory He may grant you to be strengthened with power through his Spirit in the inner person, that Christ may dwell in your hearts through faith ... (Ephesians 3:16–17)

It is important for you to understand a few things about the Holy Spirit. The Holy Spirit isn't a force. He isn't an influence. He isn't a feeling that I get. He is a person and all of Him came to live in you, at the moment of your spiritual re-birth. There are some groups that falsely teach that you need to get more of the Holy Spirit but that just doesn't line up with Scripture. The Holy Spirit is a person and you cannot get part of a person now and part of a person later. You don't get an arm when you get saved and a leg later. You have all of the Holy Spirit you are ever going to get. The problem isn't that I need more of Him; the problem is He needs to get more of me.

I'm amazed at times when a I hear a Christian pray, "Lord I just hope you'll be with us tonight." Let me ask you, Is there any chance He wouldn't be? That's not a prayer of faith, that's a prayer of unbelief. When we get ready to send our kids off to college and we stand out by the car and say, "We'd like to have a word of prayer— Lord I just hope you will go with them ..."

I always just ask, "Are they a Christian?"

"Well Yes."

"Then there's no chance He wouldn't go—He's in them! What do you mean asking Him to go with them? He's there."

The better prayer would be, "We thank you Lord that you live in us." The Truth really sets us free. Instead of begging God for what He has already given us, we can just say, "Thanks." You don't have to beg God for anything. You just thank Him for what He's done. He loves his children, He loves to spoil them. The fact that we have the Holy Spirit always present with us In Christ is just amazing.

Working on Our Condition

"... But you were washed, you were sanctified, you were justified in the name of the Lord Jesus Christ and by the Spirit of our God."(1 Corinthians 6:11)

Now there is a real danger in not understanding position and condition. *Position comes by birth.* It just happens the moment you're born, in this case, the moment you are spiritually re-born. At the moment of your spiritual new birth, your *position* changed but your *condition* did not. Your condition is changed by cooperating with the Holy Spirit and "working out your salvation with awe and reverence" as Paul says (see Philippians 2:12-13). We are not working *for* salvation—we received that fully In Christ. We are *working out* the salvation we have already received.

When you and I trusted Christ, our position changed immediately. We were raised with Christ, justified and positionally glorified. But our condition did not immediately change. One minute after your new spiritual birth, you still smelled like the world, talked like the world, thought like the world. Now it will take you the rest of your life to have your condition brought up to the level of your position.

One of the things that Jesus was most criticized for was the company he kept. He always ran around with bad people. He kept bad company. All the "religious" people told him, "You shouldn't run around with those people. Those people are prostitutes, those are tax collectors—and we really hate those tax collectors." The Pharisees decided the tax collectors couldn't be saved. They were Jews who sold out to Rome. But Jesus ran around with them. He always runs in bad company. That's how he met me. That's how he met you because it's only bad people that need The Savior.

So, every time I'm in a group of Christians, I always know I am in bad company! That should help us all relax. I don't have any false expectations about you. Please don't have any about me. The only good thing about me is that Christ lives in me. If you are In Christ, spiritually alive, then Christ also lives in you. Now that He is living in you, He wants to change you, transform you from the inside out.

When you trusted Christ, you were at that very moment positionally *sanctified*. That just means that you were "set apart" for God. You became His treasured possession. It also means that you were cleansed of your sin— "washed" as Paul says in the 1 Corinthians passage above. So *positionally* in Christ, we were Justified, Sanctified and Glorified. Now throughout the rest of our life we are going to cooperate with the Holy Spirit as He seeks to make this *conditionally* true of us. We are going to be working to bring our condition up and in line with our position.

Take a look a this chart, it will help you visualize what we are talking about:

Raised With Christ > > > > > > > > Glorified

POSITION

CONDITION *over time* **Sanctification**

Justified
(Positionally Sanctified)
*The moment of your
spiritual rebirth*

It is a tragedy that many Christians don't understand this truth and get confused and discouraged. You might look at the condition your life is in at the present moment and draw the conclusion that you are not saved, that you are not In Christ. But that is an inverted Gospel. Until we are convinced that we are raised up In Christ, we will not be able to work on our condition effectively.

If we go back to Paul for a minute and think about his letters, you may remember that he was writing to believers. In most of his letters, he would remind them of their position in Christ first, like in 1 Corinthians: "To the church of God that is in Corinth, to those *sanctified* in Christ Jesus, called to be saints together with all those who in every place call upon the name of our Lord Jesus Christ, both their Lord and ours" (1 Corinthians 1:2). He would remind them of their position in Christ—called, justified, glorified, sanctified.

Then he would turn to their condition like he does in Romans:

> I appeal to you therefore, brothers, by the mercies of God, to present your bodies as a living sacrifice, holy and acceptable to God, which is your spiritual worship" (Romans 12:1).

You see, Paul would always affirm their position before he dealt with their condition. Once you get firm in your position and you understand that's your birthright, then you can go to work on your condition without fear of losing your position. Position is established by birth—in this case your new birth In Christ. We will be spending the rest of our lives working on our condition.

When people begin to mess up, no matter what age, they come to me and they say, "Boy, my life is in a sorry condition."

I'll say, "Well, are you a Christian?"

"Oh yeah, I can tell you when Christ came to live in me."

So we reaffirm their position.

Then I say, "OK, we got that settled. Let's go to work where the problem is. The problem is the condition of your life and what you are going to do about that."

So now the question becomes, "What do you do? How do you do it?" We might even wonder, "Why does God allow this struggle? Why doesn't he just make us perfect when we're re-born? He's gonna do it in heaven anyway."

The Lord is testing and maturing our faith through the struggles that we go through. This struggle against sin is part of the trying, the testing of your faith that Peter tells us is more precious than gold (1 Peter 1:6-7).

Now you have to be completely convinced that God the Father will get you home. I'm not the least bit worried about going to heaven. I'm very excited about that but, I'm not in a big hurry. When we get to heaven, we will never fight any spiritual warfare again—no struggles, no conflict. You won't have a Sin Nature. Satan won't be there. There won't be any of the world's system, no temptation. It will be perfect righteousness. In Heaven you will never, ever win another person to Christ. All of your loved ones who are with the Lord right now have absolutely no spiritual conflict. It is incredible. It is wonderful.

But I'm not ready to go yet. I keep telling the Lord, "Don't stop yet. I've got people I want to share with, I've got places I want to go. I've still got battles to fight. I'm glad to know that whenever my battle is won, my course has run, my battle is completed, then, I'll take off—I'll be out of here. But not yet.

If you read about me dying, don't you believe it. What you're looking at in that casket, won't be me. It will just be the tent, all folded up that I used to live in. I'll be in a far, far better state.

Because, you see, it's in the trying of your faith, in that wrestling match that you are saying something to him that costs you something. In the meantime, He wants to see what you're gonna do.

Since the Holy Spirit is now living in you In Christ, a possibility exists in your life that does not exist to anyone that is In Adam. That possibility is that you can now reflect the image of God and you can bring your condition up gradually, slowly to be in line with your position. You can be progressing, spiritually maturing In Christ.

The Old Nature vs. The New Nature

Before you can make any progress in your spiritual growth, there is one more important issue that you need to understand. Back when Adam fell, he was invaded by sin and so he developed a Sin Nature. The Sin Nature is basically a disposition. The Bible calls it the Old Man, the Old Person (see Romans 6:6; Ephesians 4:22; Colossians 3:9). So when Adam thought he could get God out of his life, that he could become completely independent, he actually became enslaved to his Sin Nature.

In Adam, you also inherited the Sin Nature. All mankind has been in bondage to the Sin Nature ever since the rebellion and fall of Adam The Sin Nature is master for everyone who is still In Adam. It is that attitude in every one of us that pops up when God says "Thou shalt" and a little voice in our head says, "I will not!" And when God say, "Thou shalt not," the voice says, "Yes I will!" That's the Sin Nature talking.

The Sin Nature will never obey God. It's an attitude or disposition that is in every one of us the minute we're born. Paul calls this attitude having a "mind set on the flesh" or to live "in the flesh." Listen to what he tells us about it in Romans:

"For the mind that is set on the flesh is hostile to God, for it does not submit to God's law; indeed, it cannot. Those who are in the flesh cannot please God." (Romans 8:7–8)

Now before any of us comes to Christ, we only had the one nature—the Sin Nature. In Adam, we only had the one nature and you could think of it being hard wired within us. Anything the Sin Nature wanted to do, I did it. If we apply this to our circles they would look something like this:

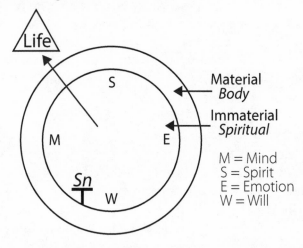

Material
Body

Immaterial
Spiritual

M = Mind
S = Spirit
E = Emotion
W = Will

But if you have trusted Christ and you are now "in Him" an amazing thing has happened: *you now have a New Nature In Christ.* If you are Alive in Christ, you now have new possibilities. This New Nature longs to please God. So when you came to Christ and the Holy Spirit placed you in the body of Christ, your position changed and you received an incredible inheritance, but you also receive a New Nature, a new empowerment that equips you to live abundantly the way God desires for you to live.

Once we became Christians, God "rewired" us, so to speak. Now In Christ, we are no longer "hard-wired" to our Sin Nature. He has broken that link and He has also given us a "wire" to our New Nature, something nobody still dead In Adam has. Lets apply this to our circles. In our circles we are going to label your Sin Nature with **Sn** and your New Nature with **Nn**. You now look like this in Christ:

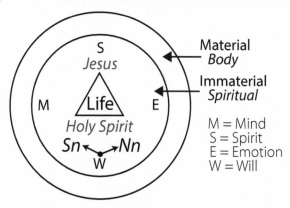

In any given situation now that you are Christian you can simply chose to serve your Old Nature and you will do the works of the flesh or you can chose to serve your New Nature and enjoy the fruits of the spirit. It's your choice. We have an option in Christ that we did not have in Adam. God has given us access to our "switch"—we can choose who we will serve.

As long as you're in your present physical body, as long as you have your Sin Nature, you will have a battle that you're going to have to fight. Your Sin Nature will be as hostile to God the day you die as the day you were born. What God desires for you is to work on bringing your *condition* up to the level of your *position*. That's the *process* called *sanctification*. We have been *positionally sanctified* In Christ—set apart for Him—and now we are being *progressively sanctified*—becoming more and more like Jesus.

Now the battle that is going on in your life and mine since the day we became Christians is not between the Holy Spirit and your Sin Nature. That's not where the battle is going on. If that's where the battle was going on the Holy Spirit could never lose but you and I lose battles every day. The battle in your spiritual life between now and glorification is between your New Nature and your Sin Nature.

Where Our Battle Lies

One of the biggest areas that I know that you and I have trouble, if we'll be honest, is our Sin Nature—our Old Self. He wants to be your master. The place where he attacks and often clobbers us is in our minds, our thoughts.

God gave you an amazing piece of engineering and that's your imagination. If I tell you to think about a banana split, you can "see" it in your mind. If I asked you to imagine a snake that's all coiled up, can you see the snake? Yes, I am sure you can, no problem. The reason God gave you that ability to form pictures in your mind is so that you could give visible expression to what God is saying in the Scriptures. He wants you to be able to "see" with your mind when He describes how beautiful and wonderful His plans are.

That's why we think in pictures. How many times have you heard someone say, "I see what you mean?" Have you ever thought about that? You keep talking until someone says, "I see it!" What is it they saw? They saw a thought. We make up images, pictures in our mind to give shape to our thoughts.

The problem is that Satan can get access to your mind through your thoughts, your imagination. It's like a big movie screen. You can be doing the dishes, driving your car, mowing the grass or working in your office and all of a sudden, without any notice, the thought will pop up, "Hey, you want to see a dirty picture?" Womp! There it is up on the screen, in 3-D and color—a huge, enormous proposition. You may be shocked and you say, "I wasn't reading pornography. I haven't watched any XXX rated movies." Now If you have been looking at those things, you are certainly going to think those thoughts. You're just helping him.

Well when that image suddenly appears, as Christians we are tempted to say, "I'm horrible, that's terrible." I had to go to those who tutored me right after I became a Christian and tell them, "I'm either more sensitive or I'm thinking more filth since I became a Christian than before; I don't understand."

I was so naïve I thought it was a good idea to tell them about my struggles. But some would say, "Don't discuss that around here." You see, they just didn't know how to handle it.

Satan propositions you by bringing it on the screen in your mind. If you try to switch channels, it won't happen. If you try to blot it out, it won't happen. A lot of Christians do a silly thing; they just decide to look at it for a little while before they give it up. "Let's just play with it for a little bit," they think. The problem is our Sin Nature likes to cling everything that keeps us from the things of God. Someone will tell you the cutest clean joke and you can't even remember it by supper. But if you hear a dirty joke it will stick. Isn't that incredible? That's just the way our Sin Nature works. Satan knows it.

Satan's Tacklebox

I like to bass fish. My son and I go down to the stores and we buy lures. Lures are not made to catch fish, they're made to catch fishermen. I love to go into the shop and watch men pick out lures. They all say, "I know they'll hit that!" Now I haven't a clue what a bass would hit. But we like get green and speckled things, hook those onto other things and tie it all together. Then we'll say, "Man that looks like a bad lure, I've got to have two of those!" We get boxes to put all our lures in. I mean, we'll carry big boxes, little boxes—boxes in boxes. Some of our lures we've never even thrown at a bass. We'll stand for hours and talk about lures.

Now a bass is a funny fish. A big bass won't eat for days. Once he's eaten, he's not going feed again for a while. He can be where you know he's going to be but he just isn't feeding. He's got the mentality of a cat, though, and what you have to do is agitate him. If you will agitate him, he'll hit your lure—not because he's hungry but because you agitated him. I've thrown a lure around a log or a stump where I knew a big bass was and on the 20th or 30th time he'd hit it. He didn't want to eat anything but I made him mad like a cat. I knew that if I kept throwing things in there in front of him, he would hit.

Satan has a tackle box full of lures for you. He knows what lure you'll hit. He knows which one you'll hit when you're hungry and he knows which one you'll hit if you're not. If you go throw certain things in front of a bass, you can hit him in the nose and he won't take a bite. But if you throw the right one his blood begins to boil and his old mouth opens up and Zoom! he's off.

Satan knows this too so what he does is just run those lures in front of you. The ones that bother me may not bother you so he won't throw those by me. The ones that put my blood boiling, he throws them by me all the time. Trolls them by, fast speed, slow speed, hits me in the head with them. He does that all day long. He does it for you too. .

In Matthew 5:28 Jesus said, "I tell you, that whoever looks on a woman to lust after her has committed adultery in his heart already." There are a couple of things going on here. First is the proposition. Now, a proposition is just that: a picture, a thought, a question. It is not sin, it is a proposition. It is the lure that is presented to you. When you get propositioned, do not imagine that you've sinned. You are going to be tempted until the day you die. What Jesus helps us understand is that sin doesn't occur until we consent with the proposition. So if a man sees an attractive woman (that's a proposition), he hasn't sinned until he lusts for her (that's when he voted). Sin occurs when you decide to switch over and listen to your Sin Nature, that Old Self. It is when you vote to do what the proposition is enticing you to do. You must understand what the trigger mechanism is. It's not the proposition, it's when you lust, when you choose, when you exercise your will.

What Will You Do?

So let me just give you a little clue. If I had a rattlesnake over there in the corner and I told you, "That's the meanest rattlesnake I've ever seen—He *will* bite you. He is poisonous. He will kill you." Now you walk by and he says to you, "Look, I have just eaten. I won't eat again for days. I am no threat. Don't believe what he said about me."

Now no one was ever bitten by a rattlesnake if they ran as soon as they saw it. Imagine if that rattlesnake said, "You're so far away I couldn't hit you from where I am. Just relax, stay where you are and look at me. You've got sense enough to know that I am far enough away, and I can't strike you. Just relax." So you let your guard down a little.

The next thing you know he'll say, "Look you can get a little bit closer than that. I can't hit you." Then you get a little bit closer. Pretty soon he says, "Have I not convinced you by now that I am not going to strike you." Eventually, he will talk you into touching him. When you reach over to touch, he strikes! That's the nature of a rattlesnake. That is the nature of sin.

Let me tell you a secret: the first 20 seconds of what you do with a proposition is the most critical. I mean the minute you see it you run, that's the first thing you have to do. It's when you hang around and say, "Look, I'm not gonna commit adultery, I'm just gonna play with the idea for 30 seconds." Thirty seconds a day spread over a week will be three and a half minutes. In two weeks, that will add up to seven minutes. You'll be fantasizing saying, "But I'm not really gonna do it," but you're just getting closer to the rattlesnake. Pretty soon, he'll strike. So the first thing you have to do when you see a proposition is to be smart enough to run.

The second thing you do when Satan gives you that picture is to bring Christ into the equation. Don't try to get the picture out of your mind, just bring Christ into the situation. When Satan makes the proposition and says, "Hey Tom, would you like to see a dirty picture?" Then I say, "I'm a Christian, I belong to Christ and I have to ask him if this is good for me. So if you don't mind let me bring Him into the equation: "Lord, is this something that would make me more like you; is this going to help me reflect your image?"

You see now I've prayed. I've brought Christ into the situation, into the proposition. The last thing Satan wants to do is to teach you how to pray, so guess what he'll do? He'll take his dirty picture away because he doesn't want to teach you how to pray better. Every time he shows me a dirty picture, I say, "Boy I am so glad you showed me that. It reminds me that I haven't talked to Christ yet today, "Lord, he showed me another dirty picture. I just wanted to thank you that I have victory even though I can't stop these pictures popping up in my thoughts. I just wanted to bring you in—What do you think about this?"

Practice the presence of Christ and begin to pray and begin to thank Him, "Lord, I know that I'm in the battle and I know what a lure is and he's running that lure by me. It's the one I really like, you know. It's the one he's always running by me. I just want to thank you that you've given me a New Nature and I want to praise you because you have given me another option." Satan doesn't want to help you grow and so he'll get off your back.

The third thing you can do is add another thought picture to your mind. You cannot erase the picture that Satan has got on your mind, but you can add one. So, you just add an image of Christ on the Cross. You can always add another image and think about two. This is what you can do to deal with the propositions that Satan throws in front of you. Remember, a proposition is not sin; it doesn't become a sin until we act on it.

The Curve Ball

When I was playing baseball back in high school, I was a pretty good hitter, but I couldn't hit a curve ball. All the pitchers in the league found that out and pretty soon they were driving me nuts with curve balls. When the game was on the line, and I needed to be a hero, they threw me curve balls. I couldn't understand it. It made me look bad. I got real disgusted, threw my helmet, threw my bat, kicked the dirt, spit, but I still didn't hit any curve balls.

One of the coaches told me to come to the field thirty minutes early every day and for an hour on Saturday. He laid some bats down on the ground and made me stand in a little trench. He got a pitcher to throw me nothing but curve balls. He would stand beside me and say, "Don't swing the bat; I just want you to watch the picture. Here comes a curve ball. It looks like it's going to hit you on the head but it isn't." He helped me to slow things down and get the picture of what was going on. Pretty soon, my weakness became my strength; I loved curve balls.

In critical situations, I could see the pitcher start to smirk because he thought he had me pegged. I'd just smirk back thinking, "Let it rip, partner. We're fixing to annihilate you." But then a crazy thing happened. He threw me a knuckle ball! I couldn't hit knuckle balls!

That is often the way it works with temptations and propositions. The minute you learn to deal with one, the tactic changes. All of us go through it. That is why you have to know the Truth about these things and be prepared to deal with them. Satan's main goal is to keep you from believing that you are a beloved Child of God with eternal birthrights and a heavenly inheritance.

The Weapons of Our Warfare

Where does Satan attack you? In your mind, in your thoughts. That's why Paul says,

> "For though we live as human beings, we do not wage war according to human standards, for the weapons of our warfare are not human weapons, but are made powerful by God for tearing down strongholds. We tear down arguments and every arrogant obstacle that is raised up against the knowledge of God, and we take every thought captive to make it obey Christ." (2 Corinthians 10:3-5 NET)

What are strongholds? They are all those things that you thought about or did in Adam that are entrenched in your mind. They are entrenched in your memory. When we came out of Adam and into Christ, we brought that baggage with us and God knows that. Anything that is propositioned to me is either taking me closer to God or taking me away from God. That's how I know if something is good or bad. God has given us all that we need to *"take every thought captive to make it obey Christ."*

In our will, you and I hold the switch to submit either to the Sin Nature or the New Nature. You hold the switch. You cannot stop the propositions and Satan won't let up. The lures will be the very ones that drive you nuts. He won't send you the ones that are easy;

he will send the ones that give you real trouble. But In Christ, there is always a way of escape:

> No trial has overtaken you that is not faced by others. And God is faithful: He will not let you be tried beyond what you are able to bear, but with the trial will also provide a way out so that you may be able to endure it. (1 Corinthians 10:13)

If you are In Christ, the old things have passed away and new things have come. We can do all things in Christ who strengthens us. He has given us all we need to live like His glorious children, winning the battles that we face day to day through His truth and grace.

Prayer

Father I thank you for the truth that sets us free from falling into temptation. We won't get it all right every time and so we thank you for your grace that sets us free of shame. We thank you that we have a New Nature in Christ and this gives us a new option for life. We thank you that we can bring Christ into every temptation that we face so that we can deal with the propositions that are set before us. We thank you that Christ comes to live in us and we in Him. We thank you that you have welcomed us as your beloved children and have given us such a rich eternal inheritance in Christ. Help us to live according to the power of the Holy Spirit who dwells within us. In Christ's name, amen.

CHAPTER 3

The Sincere Christian

*"This is my prayer for you: that your love may abound
even more and more in knowledge and every kind of insight
so that you can decide what is best, and thus be sincere and blameless
for the day of Christ, filled with the fruit of righteousness
that comes through Jesus Christ to the glory and praise of God."*
PHILIPPIANS 1:9–11

In the height of the Roman empire, during the times of Paul and Jesus, the Roman status symbol was having an original marble statue. In your villa or in your home, be it ever so palatial or modest, you had to have statuary, an original. You would have an entry garden or a sitting garden or walking garden in the back of your home. You might have had one of those foyers inside your home. Somewhere there was a focal point where you had one of these original marble statues. They were quite expensive and that was the status symbol.

The artists that were doing those statuaries would take big blocks of marble and they would begin to form their statuary. Sometimes, they would be well into their work of art, and hit a flaw in the marble and a piece would just sheer off. There might be a piece of the hip that would just fall off. Sometimes when they were doing very delicate work around the face, they would be chiseling around the nose and the nose would sheer off or the eye socket would cave in. Of course the artist would have to stop and discard that piece. The statue was now flawed and it wouldn't sell at a high price. All of those flawed pieces got pushed to the side.

Now they had entrepreneurs running around even in Paul's day and someone thought, "Surely there's got to be a way to use those flawed and damaged statues." So they came up with a process where they took some marble from the statue, from the base or some other area, and ground it up into a powder and mixed it with wax. Then they would take that wax mixture and reform the missing parts. They could put the nose back and replace half of the ear. They could build the hip out. Since it was the original marble dust mixed with wax you couldn't see it, you couldn't tell it. So now they could sell those statues at a huge discount and nobody would really know the difference.

Of course, those discount statues became hot items. All the less "well-to-do" wanted one of those statuaries. Whenever you had guests over, the first thing you would do is sort of get them loose and then you would escort them to your private showing. Everyone would purr and say, "That's one heck of a statue!"

"Yes, and I'm sure that's expensive."

"Oh yes, that's very expensive."

"That's an original right there."

Everything would be going well, unless it was summertime. Then the heat would come and the problem would appear. Just at some critical moment in your showing while everyone was gazing, the nose would begin to slide down the face. The ear might suddenly fall off into the bushes. How embarrassing. Wax works wonders until the heat gets turned up.

God's Trophies

Imagine if you were in the first century and God took you to the early church and said, "Listen, I want you to come and see what I paid the ultimate price for. These are my trophies." When you walked in and saw the types of people the early church was made up of, corrupt tax collectors, prostitutes, some murderers, thieves —bad company just like you and me—you might have said, "Excuse me there's been a mistake. This couldn't be the right group!"

But God says, "These are my trophies." God picks up all the broken and flawed and cracked pieces of humanity and calls them His trophies. God says if you come into my trophy house—which is the church—I want you to see what I value most. What, in fact, I paid the highest possible price for. Listen to what Paul had to say:

> Think about the circumstances of your call, brothers and sisters. Not many were wise by human standards, not many were powerful, not many were born to a privileged position.
>
> But God chose what the world thinks foolish to shame the wise, and God chose what the world thinks weak to shame the strong. God chose what is low and despised in the world, what is regarded as nothing, to set aside what is regarded as something, so that no one can boast in his presence. (1 Corinthians 1:25–29)

God's trophies are not what the world puts any value on. The world looks at broken things and says that's trash and discards it. But God only cherishes those who are broken—the foolish, the weak, the low and despised—and calls us His trophies.

Waxing Up

Now a sad thing has happened in the churches. The church kind of cleaned up. It became a place for "respectable people." It became something very different from what the Lord intended. We all come to the Lord just as we are—with all our cracks, all our flaws, all our imperfections, all our blemishes, all our scars—We come knowing that God accepts us in Christ, saying "That's my child!" We come "just as we are without one plea" knowing that God accepts us that way. But then we begin to look around and think, "I don't know that I fit in here with all my mess." We begin to think, "I need to get my act together." We think we need to "wax up" in order to fit in.

We all have the tendency in our early Christian life to "wax up." We try to get all the Christian language right. We get the right kind of bible. We get our behavior all worked out—"It's OK to do this here; It's not OK to do this here." Of course we get our dress code right so that everything looks right on the outside. When it really takes hold, we are pretending to be someone we are not. But when we "wax up," we're setting ourselves up for big trouble because invariably the heat comes.

When the Heat is Up

This "heat" of life is what I call God's reality check. God has this amazing way of melting wax. He allows the heat to get turned up on us because he realizes that the wax—the pretending—is what keeps you from seeing how much you need Him. We all give the perception that we really don't need anything until the heat comes. That's when we are moved to say, "I need prayer. I need your help. I need somebody to lift me up in this time of sadness and in sorrow."

When the heat of real life suddenly comes crashing down on us in a blinding moment, that's when we find out just how much reality there is in our lives. This is the kind of heat that comes when we find out our teenage daughter is pregnant, or our son is addicted to drugs, or our marriage is in real trouble. It's when the heat comes that the wax will melt and the flaws will be exposed.

It's only when all the wax comes off and all the veneer is peeled away and we're down to reality that we ever sincerely seek God. He loves us too much to let us be fake. God also melts our "wax" so that we will never have any cause to boast in His presence. It is important for you to know that God isn't as interested in your image as He is in His image. He isn't so interested in your reputation as He is in your relationship with Him. He isn't as interested in your ability as He is in your availability to Him. What God wants is sincere Christians. God desires beyond all else to have an intimate relationship with every one of his children.

We all desire intimacy, whether it's our relationship with God, our spouse, or a friend. The essential agreement in intimacy is transparency. Transparency is absolutely required for there to be intimacy. I have to be totally transparent with another person, with my wife, with my children, with God. To be transparent means you have to get rid of the "wax." When the wax is gone, we begin to enter into transparency or sincerity. In our relationship with God, this means that we begin to see things as He sees things.

He says,

> "Listen I knew about all those cracks, I knew about all those failures, I knew about all those imperfections when I adopted you into my family. If I accepted you initially as you were why do you need to wax up? Not for me. I called you a trophy the day I called you to myself. Why do you need to wax up? Certainly not for me! With all that wax, you're not real. And with all that wax you're not free. You're not free to be who I want you to be because you've got this waxed up image. You're trying to be what you're not and as long as you are doing this you are not free. Being free is your greatest asset."

The Divine Audit

Now I was in the business world for much of my life and we used to have these things called audits. One of the documents that auditors use is a balance sheet and it simply lists your assets and liabilities. One day I wondered, "What would happen if God conducted a Divine Audit on my life? What would my balance sheet look like?" The answer I discovered was interesting.

We know that God's ways are not our ways—He looks at things very differently. In reading the Scriptures, I have become convinced that *what we often think of as an asset, God considers a liability*. The reason He considers it a liability is because often what we perceive as our assets keeps us from needing Him. Have you ever thought about that?

Your liabilities are the things that frighten you, terrify you, bring you anxiety. But these "liabilities" drive you to God. Those are the things that bring you to Him. So you see our "liabilities" become our greatest assets—they drive us to God, to depend on Him.

So how does God give us an audit? He turns the heat on. That's your reality check. The heat shows whether something is real or fake.

I want you to listen to what I'm going to tell you very carefully. Your Bible will not be truly precious to you until you survive the heat and the pain of life through all the truth it contains. It is not until the Truth of the Word has become reality in your experience that you'll say, "His Word is life to me." Before the heat comes, the Truth is just words on a printed page. For the Written Word to become the Living Word in your life, God has to take you through the heat—the pain, the suffering—so that you can experience and claim His truth as your own. You hang on to the Truth and you discover that it is true and it carries you through.

When the Heat is On

I'd like to give you some things to think about the next time the heat's on. Maybe you are there now and you need help.

First of all, you need to know and be convinced that God is in control and He's sovereign over everything. He knows what is going on with you and is concerned about your situation. You have to hang on to that. Jesus taught us, "

> Are not two sparrows sold for a cent? And yet not one of them will fall to the ground apart from your Father. But the very hairs of your head are all numbered. Therefore do not fear; you are of more value than many sparrows.
>
> Matthew 10:29–31

Secondly, God loves His children. Sometimes as I am asking God to give someone I love relief, I too am hurting because they're hurting. It suddenly dawned on me that God loves my loved one more than me and He aches with us both. He loves those who ache with those who ache.

The third thing is He will never give you more than you can bear. You might think it is, but it isn't. He is going to use every pain and every struggle and every hurt and everything you have to go through for your good:

> And we know that all things work together for good for those who love God, who are called according to His purpose …
> Romans 8:28

God is working everything that we go through for our good, even if we don't understand it at the time.

The fourth truth that we hang on to is that our greatest and highest goal in this life is to get to know Him. Whatever I'm going through is going to be used by God to help me know him better. It's gonna melt the wax, expose my need, drive me to Him and I'll come out of it knowing Him better. That's His greatest goal even when you're crushed with pain and fear and anxiety and frustration.

The writer of Hebrews tells us,

> My son, do not scorn the Lord's discipline or give up when he corrects you. For the Lord disciplines the one he loves and chastises every son he accepts...
>
> Endure your suffering as discipline; God is treating you as sons … Besides, we have experienced discipline from our earthly fathers and we respected them; shall we not submit ourselves all the more to the Father of spirits and receive life? For they disciplined us for a little while as seemed good to them, but he does so for our benefit, that we may share His holiness. Hebrews 12:5–10 NET

God brings pain into our lives as discipline, to grow us up so that we may know Him and share in His holiness! What an amazing thought!

Just remember in all things, God is working to bring you closer to Him. Now, when you're going through the pain, you can remember all these truths. You can write them down in the margin of your Bible. There are times when the pains are so intense that the Lord's purposes are not understandable. At times you will repeat these truths to yourself and they don't seem to help.

Sometimes it takes years before you comprehend a tragedy or a trauma that happened in your life. It doesn't always show up the moment you're going through it. When you're in that never-never land—in the place where the pain and the mysteries and the traumas happen—you have to cling to one thing: *God is with you in the pain.* God will be with me after the pain, and I don't know when, but I will see that God knew what He was doing. That Truth is the main thing that will get us through.

We need to remind ourselves that we are the bride of Christ and He's the groom. We are not always the faithful bride but He is always the faithful groom. One of the things that keeps me anchored when all the pain, pressure, and heartache is going on around me is just to remember that when Christ made His vows to me and you, He promises to never leave nor forsake us (see Hebrews 13:5). He's the faithful groom.

People generally don't come to my office to tell me good news. Almost every time I get a call, it's like a call to the paramedics. They always get called to scenes of accidents and where somebody has been hurt. So we automatically know when the phone rings somebody is hurting.

Do you know what it is like to be around a person who is racked with pain. You've heard that little phrase—"racked with pain"? Let me tell you what my definition of racked with pain is: It's when you are going through something that is hard to understand and it's hard to endure. You think, "I don't know whether I'm going to make it."

It's not just the person hurting that is racked with pain. When my children hurt, I'm racked with pain. Whether it's physical pain or emotional pain; when they hurt, I hurt. When it's somebody that's very close to me, that I love very deeply, that is when it is the hardest. But because I know the Truth, I am secure. Because I know the Truth, I can share that Truth so that others can find help and comfort.

The Real Role Models
The Apostles were the "heavy hitters," in the early church. Sometimes, people would hold them up on pedestals as "Super-Christians." They

were role models, but they were also sincere Christians. One of the things that you have to realize is that the Apostles were men who lived in the reality of life. Listen to this,

> God has exhibited us apostles last of all, as men condemned to die, because we have become a spectacle to the world, both to angels and to people.   1 Corinthians 4:9 NET

Paul says that God had chosen to make the Apostles last and that they were a spectacle to the world and also to the angels. The world looks at the Apostles and says, "What kind of leaders are these?" The angels look upon the Apostles and say, "If these are Gods leaders, what a joke!"

Nobody really wanted to be an Apostle. They were stoned, beaten, ship wrecked, starved, hunted, and condemned to die, as Paul says. Nobody wanted the office of an Apostle. But these were some of God's trophies.

In another place Paul says,

> When I came to you, brothers and sisters, I did not come with superior eloquence or wisdom as I proclaimed the testimony of God. For I decided to be concerned about nothing among you except Jesus Christ, and him crucified. And I was with you in weakness and in fear and with much trembling. My conversation and my preaching were not with persuasive words of wisdom, but with a demonstration of the Spirit and of power, so that your faith would not be based on human wisdom but on the power of God.
>
> 1 Corinthians 2:1–5 NET

Paul and the other Apostles knew what it means to suffer. They faced fear, weakness, sickness, even doubt. But they became examples of Sincere Christians. There was no wax. In all their brokenness, God revealed His great power. In all their liabilities, God's revealed His strength.

A sincere Christian is one who realizes that they are broken. A sincere Christian is someone has not filled their life with the wax of unreality. When the heat comes, they are able to endure because their life is built on the Truth. I want you to know that God's trophies are un-waxed, sincere Christians because when a non-Christian is around a sincere Christian, he or she says, "Maybe there's hope for me. *Maybe there's hope for me.*"

I'll tell you when the heat is on, every waxed-up Christian will run and try to find a sincere Christian. They're gonna hunt you. They may stay waxed until the heat comes but when comes, they are going to be exposed. A sincere Christian knows Christ. He's been in the fire. He or she knows what it is to be stripped until they say, "Listen, what you see is what you get; but for the grace of God, I wouldn't be standing here." God can use people like that. He wants you to be a Sincere Christian so that even if you are a spectacle to the world, you will be a trophy to Him.

Prayer

Father, we thank you for the truth that sets us free from being fake, "waxed-up" Christians. You're looking at us and you know each of us intimately. You know what we need to be whole even if we don't. Even though we don't want anyone to suffer, we thank you that you raise the heat in our lives so that the wax will melt away. We thank you for just reminding us that when we come into your presence we want to have more reality than wax. Help us to know this truth so that we may give comfort to others when they are facing the heat. In Christ's name. Amen.

CHAPTER 4

Finding Fulfillment

*The path of the righteous
is like the bright morning light,
growing brighter and brighter until full day.
The way of the wicked is like gloomy darkness;
they do not know what causes them to stumble.*
PROVERBS 4:14–19

There is a question that has preoccupied the young, the old—entire societies and cultures—since the beginning: "How do I find fulfillment in life?" Our culture is currently obsessed with this question though the answer seems hard to find. We have more options promising us fulfillment today than ever before and yet we have a social and cultural crisis on our hands.

We have a divorce rate like no other country in the world. We have broken homes, single parents, and frustrated families. We have abortion that is out of control. We have all kinds of gender confusion today. People can't figure out which side they're on or where they want to be. Sexual abuse has become epidemic. Pornography and all types of explicit material can be found almost anywhere. You can see what it's costing us in society and you can also hear the cries of people who have been hurt and damaged. We are all looking for fulfillment, but our culture shows us that very few are finding it.

Suspicion has replaced trust in this country. We now tell our grandchildren and our children, "Be careful. Don't trust anyone—not even family; you have to be on guard." By sowing that into the hearts of children, they fear adults. We've scared them to death. Adults are hesitant to protect and nurture our children for fear that someone might perceive them as child molesters. Teachers have to be very cautious. Childcare workers are paranoid. Pastors and Counselors are scared that every time they have a counseling session, someone is going to claim that they have been violated in some way.

I would like to discuss the question, "How do we find true fulfillment?" I want you to understand what it is and the bright prospects that await anyone who discovers the truth about this topic. Right up front, I want you to know that true fulfillment is found when we follow the Way of Wisdom.

What is True Wisdom?

So what is wisdom? What you need to know first is there are basically two approaches to life; one we will call the way of Worldly "Wisdom" and the other the way of Godly Wisdom. I have put worldly "wisdom" in quotes, because I want you to know that this "wisdom" is not really wisdom at all and it cannot deliver what it promises: the good life, the fulfilled life.

True wisdom is the skill to live life from God's point of view, and that is what we are calling Godly Wisdom. You can't get this kind of wisdom genetically and you can't get it by just hanging around for 50 or 80 years. Wisdom is something you learn, like a job skill, and you get it by sitting at the seat of the Father, allowing the Holy Spirit to teach you in all the arenas of life. The key issue in learning True, Godly Wisdom and finding fulfillment is knowing the Truth. The Truth always sets us free.

What is Worldly "Wisdom"?

> "When people seek a taste of heaven by their own means,
> they create a living hell of uncontrollable desires."
>
> (Harry Schaumberg, *False Intimacy*)

Worldly "wisdom" is always the current popular philosophy and approach to life. We see it illustrated in programs on TV and the radio, the books and newspapers we read, and in movies.

It wasn't long ago that a beer company had the slogan, "You only go around once, so you ought to live it with all the *gusto* you can." *Gusto* was represented by drinking their beer, with a certain group of people, in a certain place. There were commercials with men sitting around a fire drinking beer saying, "You know, it doesn't get any better than this." That is the view of the World—it doesn't get any better than sitting around the fire with some friends drinking beer. Well I have tried that and I've often said to my children, "If it doesn't get any better than that, we're in trouble!"

Our culture has created a whole industry—marketing and advertising—that calls us to try to find this fulfillment we're looking for in the products that they offer. They create a real need in your life or a fancied "need" and then promise you fulfillment—"We have exactly what you need!" I'm almost convinced that if you don't brush your teeth with a certain type of toothpaste with the right kind of fluoride, your wife won't kiss you!

There is a tremendous amount of advertising going on promising fulfillment. It's a business that exploits the fact that people have an unfulfilled life. So the advertisers come in and say, "We know what you need and we have it! Just buy our stuff." So we have all of these options offered to us to find fulfillment in every area of life, and yet everybody is still looking.

The root problem with this worldly philosophy is failing to distinguish between *needs* and *wants*. We have true needs—desires that really need to be fulfilled. But we also have desires that do not have to be fulfilled. The media and the world seek to misdirect our desires and then promise us fulfillment for those desires.

You and I have enough sense to know that when we feel thirsty that we need to get a drink of water. This is a desire that is also a real need; without water we would die. When you get hungry, you have enough sense to know you need to get some food. When you get tired you know you need to find fulfillment in a good night's rest.

It's an easy step from those three basic needs to believing that if I feel unfulfilled in *any* area of my life, then I need to get satisfaction. At this point, the world will offer us a new experience, a new relationship—something to satisfy that new "need." But what the World offers never really provides fulfillment. What worldly "wisdom" really offers us is what the Bible calls idolatry. That is the real problem. Idolatry is the worship of anything or anybody other than the One True God.

You and I were designed by God for desire. We have all kinds of desires and all of these are linked to our deep longing to be totally fulfilled as a creature of God. If that desire is misdirected, which is what the world and Satan tempt us to, then we have a problem. When you and I develop a desire or passion for anything that God says will never fulfill us, that passion or desire becomes an idol. It becomes our substitute for God.

Idolatry takes root in our misdirected desires. Instead of hungering and thirsting for God and His goodness, His righteousness, we begin to hunger and thirst after our passions, after our desires—what we perceive to be our needs. When those perceived desires become stronger than our desire for God Himself, we will discover that we will never be truly fulfilled.

I want to ask you a question that I've asked myself: "How do you know when a desire is an idol?" The answer is fairly simple: an idolatrous desire is any desire that moves you away from God. A valid desire will always take you towards God, deepening your relationship with Him.

What is Godly Wisdom?

That leads us to our second approach to life, the Way of Godly Wisdom. It is Godly because it comes from God Himself. It answers the question, "What does God have to say about life and fulfillment?"

In Psalms 37:4 David says,

> Delight yourself in the Lord
> and he will give you the desires of your heart.

Delight yourself in the Lord. Have a passion for God and He will give you the desires of your heart. This doesn't mean He will give you everything you *want*, but it does mean He will give you what you *need*. Those "heart desires" are often so deep within us that we don't even know what they really are. The Lord does and He will fulfill those true needs.

Psalm 73 was written by a man named Asaph. He's well worth you getting to know. Asaph really complains in Psalms 73. He looked at the ungodly and he said, "Life is unfair. God doesn't seem to be doing anything about it." Asaph had become disillusioned. He is essentially asking, "What benefits are there for a person who tries to make God their passion and their desire?" Asaph learned some things in this process. He shared them in the Psalm. In verse 25, this is what he said:

> Whom have I in heaven but you Lord
> and there is none upon the earth that I desire
> besides You.

Asaph was a wise king and he tells us that in his life-journey nothing in Heaven or on Earth could fulfill the longing of his heart other than his relationship with God Himself. There is no social, sexual, or financial offering that will ever bring us total fulfillment; only by delighting in the Lord will we find this fulfillment. Once you seek the kingdom of God first, as Jesus says, then all other things will be added to you (see Matthew 6:33). In other words, it's when God is in His rightful place in your heart that you will be fulfilled.

Laying A Wise Foundation: The Past

I want you to think about a building, any building: a house, your office building, any building that comes to mind. Before any building starts, there are a lot of things that have to happen. People have to plan, money has to be raised, an architect has to be hired, a builder must be contracted. Now after the site is prepared, but before the building can be built, the very first thing that has to be laid is the foundation.

If you asked me after the foundation is laid, "Tom how big do you think this building is going to be?" I can tell you exactly how big it is going to be. *The building could only be as big as the limits of the foundation.* Builders don't pour foundations and then build outside or inside the dimension of the foundation; they build it to match the foundation.

Now I want you to hear from the wisest man who ever lived (other than the Lord Jesus), a man named Solomon. In Proverbs 4 Solomon gives us instruction about wisdom and how to lay a foundation of Godly Wisdom in our lives. There are three components to this foundation that we are going to discuss: Be Teachable, Be Willing to Obey and Seek Wisdom. All of these are necessary to having bright prospects for your future.

Component One: Be Teachable

Proverbs 4:1-3
1 Hear, children, a father's instruction,
     and be attentive, that you may gain insight,
2 for I give you good precepts;
     do not forsake my teaching.
3 When I was a son with my father, tender,
     the only one in the sight of my mother.

Solomon said, "Listen to me my children." He wasn't a young man by the time he wrote this; he was in his fifties. Solomon at that point was a product of his past; the foundation for his life was laid in his past. We are all, in fact, products of our past—the foundation for our lives has been laid by what we have already experienced.

So he says, "Listen to me and hear a fathers' teaching." Solomon goes on to say that he had good things to teach, things that he had learned from his father. King David taught Solomon and told him to let his heart receive his wise teaching and follow the commands that he gave him. Solomon passes that instruction along to us.

Solomon said that he was teachable because he was young, a son to his father, an only child to his mother. He is saying, "My teachableness from a child and through my learning years is what prepared me for what God has given me now."

Now some of us may not have had particularly wise fathers to instruct us in the way of wisdom like Solomon did. The good news is, it is never too late to start learning! Solomon has recorded his wisdom in the book of Proverbs for us and that is a good place to start to learn the way of Godly Wisdom.

How teachable are you?

Component Two: Be Willing to Obey

Proverbs 4:4
[My father] taught me and said to me,
"Let your heart hold fast my words;
keep my commandments, and live.

The second component is willingness to obey his father's instruction. *It's one thing to know wisdom but it is another thing to follow and obey that instruction.* David told Solomon to hold his words fast in his heart and to keep his commandments. In order for David's wisdom to have effect in Solomon's life, he would have to do what his father passed on to him.

David, who had been instructed in the way of wisdom, passed that wisdom along to his son Solomon because he wanted Solomon to live life to the fullest. Solomon is telling us to follow wise instruction and in doing so, we won't miss anything. We'll max out. We'll be fulfilled. We will learn how to really live.

It's very unpopular today to be obedient. Everybody wants to be independent and rebellious. Everybody wants to resist any kind of authority. They resent it when anybody tries to tell them anything today. Solomon says that learning to obey wise instruction is key to life. Obedience doesn't lead to less in life, but a more fulfilled life.

How willing are you to be obedient to wise instruction?

Component Three: Seek Wisdom

Proverbs 4:5-7

5 Get wisdom; get insight; do not forget,
    and do not turn away from the words of my mouth.
6 Do not forsake her, and she will keep you;
    love her, and she will guard you.
7 The beginning of wisdom is this:
    Get wisdom, and whatever you get, get insight."

Now in verses 5-7 Solomon tells us to get Wisdom because she will not disappoint, she will keep us and guard us. David and Solomon were men principled by wisdom and that made the difference. Solomon tells us that knowing that you need to get wisdom is the beginning of wisdom! Knowing we need wisdom is the first step in getting to it.

Solomon tells us to not get distracted, don't turn away, don't forget that getting wisdom is of principal importance in our lives. We should be careful not to let anyone or anything misdirect our desires. Don't be turned away from the words of God's wise instruction. Because wisdom is from God, when we get wisdom, we get closer to Him. True wisdom leads us to God.

I want you to consider a question I have had to ponder: *"What is the principal pursuit in your life?"* Let me tell you something that will help you figure out what the principal thing in your life is: It's the thing you would tell your child to do most of all.

You may tell your child, "Be sure you get a college education." If the child were to ask you why, you might say, "So you can make money." So now you discover that the principal thing is to make money. But in God's Way of Wisdom that isn't the principal thing. We have a lot of people who have made a lot of money and they're not fulfilled. They're miserable. Their marriages are in all kinds of trouble. So the true principal thing is not to just make money.

An education doesn't do anything unless you know what to do with your education. You can't know what to do with your education so that it will produce a fulfilled life if you don't have true godly wisdom. So you may get an education and make money apart from God's wisdom and then you wonder, "Why am I so unfulfilled?" There is nothing wrong with getting an education or making money, but until we have wisdom, we won't know how to manage either of those things.

What is your principal pursuit in life?

Are you seeking true wisdom?

Building on The Wise Foundation: The Present

In Proverbs 4, Solomon said that his past laid the foundation for his present. He then talks about his present situation. That's the second thing that I want you to consider. He tells us that where we are headed in the future is a result of the course we are setting right now. So we lay the foundation of getting wisdom and now we begin to raise the building. We move up with the next level. Look at the next several verses.

> Proverbs 4:10-13|
> 10 Listen, my child, and accept my words,
>   so that the years of your life will be many.
> 11 I will guide you in the way of wisdom and
>   I will lead you in upright paths.
> 12 When you walk, your steps will not be hampered,
>   and when you run, you will not stumble.
> 13 Hold on to instruction, do not let it go;
>   protect it, because it is your life.

Solomon calls us to accept his words and instruction as from a wise father. He provides a role model. He walked in the way of wisdom and discovered that it was the key to a long and fulfilled life. When you walk in the way of wisdom, your steps won't be hindered. When you run, you're not going to stumble and fall. In the way of Wisdom you have bright prospects for your future. You can be genuinely excited about life. Again he says "take hold of wise instruction and protect it because it is your life." The way to a fulfilled life is a life lived out of God's wisdom.

Now beginning in verse 14, Solomon give us a few warnings and we want to look at those now.

Avoid the Way of the Wicked

> Proverbs 4:14 -19
> 14 Do not enter the path of the wicked
>   or walk in the way of those who are evil.
> 15 Avoid it, do not go on it; turn away from it, and go on.
> 16 For they cannot sleep unless they cause harm;
>   they are robbed of sleep
>   until they make someone stumble.
> 17 For they eat bread gained from wickedness
>   and drink wine obtained from violence ...
> 19 The way of the wicked is like gloomy darkness;
>   they do not know what causes them to stumble.

Basically, Solomon is telling us to avoid all the ways of the wicked and those who are evil. Let me give you the simple definition of evil: It's anything that takes you away from God and his wisdom. Nothing complicated about that. If something takes you away from God it's not of God and it will never lead to fulfillment.

Solomon says the wicked cannot sleep unless they are doing evil. They stay up all night figuring out how to cause harm. An evil person has no interest in God. He isn't interested in anything that takes him toward God. He's interested only in those things that take him away from God. The wicked get their "fulfillment" out of their twisted, violent schemes. Solomon says, "Stay away from all this! It's end is gloomy darkness!"

Guard Your Principles, Guard Your Heart

Proverbs 4:20-23

20 My child, pay attention to my words;
  listen attentively to my sayings.
21 Do not let them depart from your sight,
  guard them within your heart;
22 for they are life to those who find them
  and healing to one's entire body.
23 Guard your heart with all vigilance,
  for from it are the sources of life.

Now Solomon tells us there has to be a consistent application of these principles. If I make a commitment to know God and His wisdom first and to avoid those who have no interest in those commitments, then I should guard all those.

In verse 23, Solomon says "you ought to guard your heart with all diligence." Your heart is the very center of your existence—all your life flows from your heart. It's what drives you. So you need to protect your heart. You should be careful about what you expose your heart to. There are things to watch and read which affect you deeply. So in wisdom, you ought to protect your heart.

Remove All Deception

Proverbs 4:24

Remove perverse speech from your mouth;
  keep devious talk far from your lips.

Solomon tells us to clean up our mouths. Stay away from filthy language and deceit—these aren't good for anybody. Being deceitful is lying and also just trying to put on a good front. It's not being *sincere*.

If you're not following God and if He isn't your number one passion and you're not being fulfilled, then you will say whatever you have to say to cover your trail. All the time it will be perverse and deceitful. There's no fulfillment in that. Jesus said: "out of the abundance of the heart, the mouth speaks" (see Luke 6:45). The minute you open your mouth, you expose your heart. The minute you talk about what's important in your life, you expose your heart.

Stay Focused Ahead

> Proverbs 4:25-27
> 25 Let your eyes look directly in front of you
>   and let your gaze look straight before you.
> 4:26 Make the path for your feet level,
>   so that all your ways may be established.
> 4:27 Do not turn to the right or to the left;
>   turn yourself away from evil.

Lastly, Solomon tells us just to keep looking ahead and make the path level. Keep our eyes fixed on the bright prospects for our future. Remember where we are heading. We don't let our eyes roam all about—that is an indication that we have not made a firm commitment to follow the way of wisdom. Instead, we look ahead keeping focused on the main objective: knowing God and His wisdom. We don't wander around, we know where we are heading because we are following God.

Bright Prospects for Your Future

Now if we take Solomon's instruction and continue following the way of God's wisdom, we are going to have bright prospects for a fulfilled life. Solomon sums all of this up where he says, "*The path of the righteous is like the bright morning light, growing brighter and brighter until full day* (Proverbs 4:18)."

I have talked with many people who say, "I've tried cars and money. I've pushed the envelope; I've known no barriers. I've defied all authorities. I've fought my own way. I've done all that and I am still miserable. Is this all there is?" What a great opportunity! I tell them, "Oh, no. That's not all there is. You've missed the whole object of the exercise." What is amazing is that at this point they are usually ready and willing to listen.

Do you remember the old RCA-Victor ad that had the dog leaning towards the old phonograph listening with his ear held up? That dog is "inclining his ear"—he is holding it up in such a way that he can hear clearly. At the bottom of the add it simply said, "His masters voice." You see the dog recognized his master's voice coming through the phonograph.

So I want to ask you, "Who do you listen to all day?" In his wisdom Solomon tells us to incline our ears toward our Master's voice.

You see in life there are two voices talking all the time. Both of those voices are promising us fulfillment. We can think about these

two voices and what they might say about marriage. The voice of the world is saying, "Do what you want; have an extramarital affair or whatever. It's OK. You ought to do this and be liberated, be free." But there's another voice saying, "My son there is fulfillment, *but not* in the ways of the world." These two voices are saying totally opposite things about the same topic. This worldly voice is saying you can find fulfillment outside your marriage. This voice of God's wisdom is saying you will only find fulfillment in being faithful to your marriage.

Now the calling of these voices isn't going to stop and you will have to make a choice which one you will follow. God has given us incredible freedom in choosing our path. You cannot choose the outcome and consequences of your choices, that's already been determined. You cannot make a wrong choice and have it turn out right. That's just the way the real world that God has designed works. What you sow, you reap. However, we can choose to follow the way of Worldly "wisdom" or the way of Godly wisdom. Only the way of Godly wisdom will lead to fulfillment.

Choosing the Right Way

Everybody's trying to convince us of how complex life can be. But from God's perspective, life isn't nearly as complex as people make it. Basically you can think of life this way: You can either make your journey with God or without Him. That is as simple as it gets.

If you were to leave Memphis and head *east* on I-40, you are not going to wind up in Little Rock, Arkansas which is *west* of Memphis. Once you make the choice to go East, you cannot at the same time head West. So it is in life: *you can go with or without God, but you can't do both.* It is a simple choice, but there will be consequences.

If you want an indication of where you'll be 5 years from now, just think about where you have come from and where you are today. Where you are today is where you will be tomorrow if nothing changes. Where you are this year will be where you are next year if nothing changes.

You are the product of your past but that doesn't have to determine who you are today, especially if your past has been bad or even if you have been making bad decisions in the present. And that is where some good news comes in. *You can change things now that will open up bright prospects for the future.*

The amazing thing is that if I make a wrong choice, I have the ability to change that choice and head in a different direction. So if I am heading east on I-40 and I realize that I really wanted to get to Little Rock, then I can just turn around, as long as I'm not too pig-headed and stubborn. I have some ground to recover but I can eventually get back to the right path. That's the good news: *God gives us the opportunity to get back on the right path.*

If you really want to be different—by different I mean fulfilled in an unfulfilled world—then the first step is getting on board with God. You will have to decide to follow His way of Wisdom. You can't change your past, but you can look at where you have come from, offer yourself to God and say, "I want to change my direction."

You may have to start laying your foundation today. You might say, "God, I want to have a teachable heart. I am willing to be obedient and follow you. I desire to seek your wisdom and be guided by it." Once you have laid that foundation, you build on it.

The only place I can honestly tell you where to find fulfillment is the last place anybody wants to look. It's in a personal, one-on-one relationship with the One who created you. He loves you so much that He won't let you be fulfilled until you are completely safe and secure in His arms. He loves you that much. He grieves for you if you have settled for lesser passions. You'll never, ever be satisfied until you're satisfied with Him. That's why he created you. You don't have to wait to get to Heaven to experience that. We can experience it right now.

The minute you give yourself to God in this way, you can be assured that He will make good on His Word: "Delight yourself in the Lord and He will give you the desires of your heart."

Prayer

Father I thank you for your truth that sets us free from the so called "wisdom" of the World. We thank you for Solomon's instruction in your way of Wisdom. Father teach us to keep our eyes focused on the things You focus on. Father, teach us to protect our hearts. Father, teach us to keep our paths straight and to keep free from deceit. Father teach us to delight in You. We want to follow Your wise path. We want to incline our ears to hear Your voice. We want to hunger and thirst for You. In Christ's Name, Amen.

CHAPTER 5

Sailing Into the Wind

The fear of the LORD is the beginning of knowledge;
fools despise wisdom and instruction.
Proverbs 1:6–7

I was in San Diego just a few months ago and in the harbor there were sailboats everywhere—big ones, middle sized ones and the little one man boats. I just stood there and watched them for a while. All the sailors in the one-man boats were constantly making adjustments. No sooner would he get the sail, the rudder and his body like he wanted them, that all the conditions would change and he would have to move everything. I figured out that there's no autopilot on a sailboat. As all of these forces were working against him, you would see him begin to get off course but then correct to get things heading the right way again. He'd correct because he knows how to balance all those contradictory forces.

I don't know whether any of you have ever sailed. Sailing is not easy, particularly if it's in a little one man skiff. Now I want you to imagine that you are sitting in a boat at a dock. You are about to leave the dock and head out into open water, navigating toward your objective.

All of this looks simple so far. But then the tide starts to go out. Soon the wind is blowing against you; the current is moving one way, the wind is blowing you in another. Suddenly, what looked so simple becomes hard. There are contradictory forces out there, the wind, the current, the tide, rocks—all kinds of things.

If we watch as a novice sailor heads out, they may be going along OK for a bit and then the wind might blow them into the rocks. They may just drift out to sea a while only to have a huge wave come and capsize the boat. For most of us, that is what life really looks like when we are first starting out. We think, "I knew exactly where I was going and I don't know what happened. I've been on the rocks, I've been upside down."

If we took a skilled sailor and we put him in that same boat, he would be able to navigate the currents, avoid the rocks, know how to deal with waves and eventually get the boat to his destination. A skilled sailor knows how to use his rudder, body weight and sail to balance contradictory forces. It looks effortless. What makes the difference for the skilled sailor and the novice? It's the same boat, same weather conditions, same problems, and same forces. It is simple: The skilled sailor has wisdom. The skilled sailor has learned to balance contradictory forces. A skilled sailor can sail into the wind and against the tide.

Just like a sailor needs skill in sailing, we all need skill in knowing how to live life. Wisdom is what we are going to focus on. In order to do that we are going to learn from one of the wisest men who ever lived—Solomon.

Solomon's Wisdom

When Solomon was young, God asked him, "If you could have any desire of your heart, what would it be?" Solomon could have asked for wealth, he could have asked for fame, he could have asked for anything you can imagine. But Solomon said, "I would like to have the wisdom to function where you've placed me as King of Israel." God was very pleased with Solomon's heart, so not only did he make Solomon the wisest man that ever lived (besides Jesus), but He also gave Solomon all the riches, fame and recognition as well.

Now Solomon started out right but he ended wrong. Solomon, even with all of his wisdom, wound up playing the fool. Solomon had the mind to think up things that you and I cannot even conceive, the power to do things you and I can't and the money to do things we can only dream of. But when he had explored how far all these things could take him, he actually became a fool. He walked away from God, wound up with 300 wives and offered his own children to idols. When Solomon reflected on all this in the book of Ecclesiastes he said, "All is vain—all is vain."

But Solomon also gave us the book of Proverbs. There, Solomon seeks to give us his wisdom. The first nine chapters of the book of Proverbs is a letter that Solomon is writing to his son but he is also writing it to us as his spiritual children. He gives all the reasons why a young man should focus all of his life on getting wisdom or the skill to live. He spends the first nine chapters presenting a case so that he can explain to a young man or to a young woman the advantages of seeing life from God's point of view.

We are not born with wisdom and it's not inherited. *Wisdom is a skill*. If you work in a trade and you are very good at that trade, then the Bible would say you have wisdom in that trade. You have a skill. Wisdom is skill for living. It's a skill for knowing how to deal with life from God's perspective.

James tells us, "If any of you lacks wisdom, let him ask God, who gives generously to all without reproach, and it will be given him" (James 1:5). Just like Solomon, we can ask God to give us wisdom. We can say, God, "I don't have the skill to parent. I don't have the skill to be a good mate to a spouse. I don't have the skills to be a good grandparent."

When we cry out, God doesn't lop off the top of our head and pour wisdom in. The first thing He does is point us to the Scriptures. He has already given us much of His wisdom there and all we have to do is go get it.

Three Life Forces

Solomon talks to us about something I will call life forces. There are some very potent life forces that are at work in the world and have been since Solomon's day. They are forces that can blow us off course and capsize us. Solomon says that you have to recognize these life forces and learn how to balance them or you'll shipwreck.

Solomon touches on three very potent life forces that we need to know how to deal with: 1) Formative Influences, 2) Evil Enticement, and 3) Divine Proclamation. First we have to know which way these forces are taking us. Then we have to learn how to counterbalance the forces that are taking us off course. Always, we have to keep in mind exactly where we want to go.

In our ministry we have a slogan, "Make your journey worthy of your destination." If you know that you will ultimately anchor your boat in the haven of heaven, then you ought to make your journey worthy of that destination.

Formative Influences

In Proverbs 1:8-9, Solomon says,

> 8 Listen, my child, to the instruction from your father,"
>   and do not forsake the teaching from your mother.
> 9 For they will be like a graceful garland on your head,
>   and like pendants around your neck.

The first formative influence in your life is your parents. They're the first formative influence that any of us have. If you're a parent of a child, if you're a grandparent, you are the very first formative influence. The first thing I want you to notice is that it takes both parents. God insists upon a family. We're not doing very well with that in our current culture. A child who is denied both parents' influence in their life is going to shipwreck unless there is some incredible skill used by the single parent.

As the father instructs the child, the mother is most often the one who enforces what is taught. Usually the father is away at work so the mother is the one who has to lay down the law. The law that she lays down, and the law that she enforces in the home with the children, is the one that she and the father have received from God. You will not find, "Well, my wife raises the children …", anywhere in the Bible. Parenting really takes both a father and a mother.

Parents should be motivated to seek the good of their children. Good parents want to get their children into port. They don't want them to capsize. They don't want them to shipwreck. They don't want them to drift out to sea and lose a lot of time. Good parents will be an ornament of grace for their children's head and they'll be pendants about their necks. I've had a few teenagers tell me that their parents felt more like chains around their necks than pendants of grace! But that is not what God intends parents to be to their children.

You will remember the story of Joseph in the last chapters of Genesis. He was sold into slavery by his brothers. He was tempted by Potiphar's wife, but resisted and got thrown in prison. He suffered in jail for many years, but then God had him elevated to become the second most powerful man in Egypt besides Pharaoh. The Pharaoh arrayed Joseph in clothes of fine linen and he put a gold chain around his neck. That gold chain was a sign of honor, trust and responsibility. That's what parents' teaching should be to their children. If we follow their wise teaching, it will bring honor to us and to God.

Let's think about these formative influences for just a minute. You have physical, biological parents, but you also have other parents. You have cultural, historical parents as well. Those forefathers produced who we are today.

We have gotten away, in America, from our historical, political, social, economic parents. We're paying the price. I wonder sometimes who is steering the ship; it certainly isn't God. The ship of State is apparently being driven by drunks. When we listen to Congress today, it sounds like people arguing over how to rearrange the deck chairs on the Titanic. We've gotten away from our historical heritage and the parents that brought this country to the greatness that it was.

We also have spiritual parents. All of us have a grandparent, an aunt, a mother, a father, or a friend who brought you to the point you're at spiritually right now. These are all formative influences—earthly parents, cultural parents, spiritual parents—all the people who have made you what you are today. They're a tremendous influence in all our lives.

Now you have the responsibility to *evaluate* and *balance* all of these influences. Did my parents really teach me what is right? Are my spiritual parents teaching me truth and wisdom? Are cultural forces blowing me in opposite directions? God says the only way any of us can really evaluate our parents is to learn about the proclamation of God, the Word of God in the Bible. We have to know what God has to say about the truth. If you know the truth, the truth will set you free. We will take a look at that shortly.

Evil Enticements

The second force that we face is what I will call evil enticements. Solomon says,

> Proverbs 1:10
> My son, if sinners entice you,
>   do not consent.

Solomon now switches. He starts briefly with the positive influence of parents and now he switches to the evil winds that blow against us. I want to focus on that word "entice." What is an enticement? There are four things that I want you to understand about enticements.

Evil Enticements are Attractive. The first thing you have to learn about an enticement is that it's going to be incredibly attractive. If it wasn't attractive, it wouldn't be an enticement. We talked earlier about that "fishing lure"—the one you can't leave alone. An enticement is something that lures you. It may be another person who is not yours. It may be some money that's not yours. It is anything that entices you to evil—something that you cannot do with the blessing of God. It's something that you know God will not give you the "green light" for. They're a lot of things you can leave alone that are not tempting. An enticement is something that Satan and his minions know will get your attention

Evil Enticements are Cumulative. The second thing about enticements is that they are cumulative. What I mean by that is that their hold on you gets more powerful the more you play around with it. You may just play with the idea in your mind for a little bit. But if you keep this up, pretty soon you are taking the next step, getting more tangled up.

If I were to sit a strong man in a chair and then take out a little spool of sewing thread and begin to wrap it around him, he'd just look at me and say, "What are you doing?" I'd say, "Just leave me alone; I am tying you up." Well, he would laugh. I would go around three or four times and say, "I've got ya." At that point he would just rise up, pop the strings, laughing at me.

Now he would sit down and we would do the whole thing again, except this time I would wind around 9 or 10 times. He could still just jump up, break my strings, thinking, "What a silly game!" Now imagine that I could get him to sit in that chair while I wound around him a couple of hundred times, a couple of thousand times. Now when he tried to jump up and break my strings he would be in for a surprise. That one little string might not be strong by itself, but the more it is wrapped the stronger it gets. This time when I say, "Got ya!" he would say, "Yep you do!"

You see enticements are cumulative. All Satan wants you to do is think about it a little bit today, and then just a little longer tomorrow. We all have heard people say, "I never really meant it to go that far… I never intended for it to end like this …" The more you dwell on that enticement, the stronger it becomes.

If you read what Solomon says in Proverbs 1:10-19 he says that evil people will entice us to bloodshed, murder, robbery and taking advantage of the innocent. We may read that as exaggerating a little bit, but he is making the point that if you open yourself up to follow evil enticements even a little, you cannot be sure where it will all end up. He says that all of these enticements can come from a group who will try to get you to join their "fraternity." Solomon warns us to stay away from them and the path they are on—it all ends in destruction.

Evil Enticements are Compulsive. Satan knows that inside each one of us there are two things: incredible greed and incredible selfishness. By nature, we are all totally selfish; if you won't admit that, you aren't being honest. That's why I want my children to be great. Guess who gets the credit? If my wife is the ideal wife, guess who wins? If my business succeeds, guess who gets the money? If I do good teaching tonight, guess who gets the praise? Don't ever think I'm not taking care of me. If you ever ask my opinion about anything that involves me, my answer will always be in my favor because I know me. When we pray, we are telling God, "Why don't you do this? That would be good for me!"

Secondly, we're all greedy. It doesn't matter what you have. If you were to pray, "God if you would just send me $1,000 ..." If that $1000 comes in, next thing you know you are praying for $2500. The minute God fills a need our expectations and "needs" move up a little higher. That's our nature. So an enticement is usually playing on our selfishness and greed. So Solomon says, "Such are the ways of everyone who is greedy for unjust gain; it takes away the life of its possessors" (Proverbs 1:19)

Evil Enticements are Totally Destructive. The fourth thing about an enticement is that it is absolutely destructive, totally destructive. It destroys homes, marriages, lives, and ministries. Our young people today are being killed by evil enticements. They are being bombarded. Everywhere they turn in culture they're being told, "Listen this is the way you find acceptance among your peers. You have to be like this. This is the way you can really have fun. This is the way that you can get rich quick. This is the way you can have all of your desires met." Drugs, alcohol, sex. Those are real enticements to a young person and to a not so young person. These enticements tell us how to get what we want instantly: "You can have it all right now."

Deep inside we want to be accepted. We want to have all our desires fulfilled. We want some excitement in life. We want to have some fun. The World and the Devil will offer us all of these enticements and if we start to play around with the them the thread starts to wrap a little at a time, around and around ....

Solomon warns us that fulfilling our desires by the ways of the greed and selfishness will take away our life, not add to it. There is another way and that is what he leads us to now.

Divine Proclamation

The third force in life, as Solomon saw it, was the force of Divine Proclamation, what God has to say about how to live life. It's important what your parents have to say and you have to be able to recognize evil. But above all things, you have to listen to and learn from God. If you do that you will develop wisdom.

Solomon tells us,

> Proverbs 1:20–23
> 20 Wisdom cries aloud in the street,
>   in the markets she raises her voice;
> 21 at the head of the noisy streets she cries out;
>   at the entrance of the city gates she speaks:
> 22 "How long, O simple ones, will you love being simple?
>   How long will scoffers delight in their scoffing
>   and fools hate knowledge?
> 23 If you turn at my reproof,
>   behold, I will pour out my spirit to you;
>   I will make my words known to you.

Wisdom is not hidden. Wisdom is accessible to all people. God has some things that he wants to tell us. Things He knows we need to know about ourselves, about life, about fulfillment, about all the pressures, and about how to sail. God says, "You can't properly evaluate all the formative influences in your life unless you have my perspective." Therefore, God encourages us above all else to get wisdom.

Thank goodness for God's divine proclamation: *wisdom*. Wisdom cries outside; She's in the streets. She's calling to you. God wishes to teach anybody who wishes to sail wisely in life. She cries in the concourse where people go every day. She goes into the opening gates and cries, "Here am I, come to me, I will teach you skill in living."

Openly in the city she cries, "How long you simple ones?" A simple person is not someone who has a learning disability; it's someone who's gullible. This is someone who has no discernment. Wisdom calls to the scoffers. These are the ones who make fun of the Bible and God's word. They don't have time for studying the Bible—they are too busy sailing their ship! And then Wisdom calls to the fool. A fool is someone who has determined in his or her heart there is no God. A fool hates wisdom. He doesn't want to hear it. He doesn't want to think about it. He has no interest in it.

Wisdom is crying but the gullible say, "I'll just stay gullible—I love it." The scoffers all scoff and say, "Yeah, that Bible study; I'll get around to that. The truth? Yeah, I understand but I haven't got time right now—I'm too busy." The fool says, "Who needs God."

Wisdom says to them all, "You should turn at my reproof!" Reproof is the reality check. Wisdom is warning that their ship is about to capsize. If they realized that, they could all raise their hands and ask for instruction. When you begin to see things crack you ought to ask for help.

Look what wisdom says: "I will pour out my spirit to you. I will make my words known to you." Wisdom is ready to do that for anyone who is ready to show up for class. If you come and cry out, "God I don't have the skill to function in life, teach me," He will not refuse. He delights to teach His truth and wisdom to anyone willing to hear.

But look what happens if we refuse:

Proverbs 1:24 -26
24 Because I have called and you refused to listen,
    have stretched out my hand and no one has heeded,
25 because you have ignored all my counsel
    and would have none of my reproof,
26 I also will laugh at your calamity;
    I will mock when terror strikes you,

When things go wrong it is too late. When the boat finally flips over, it is too late to be worrying about sailing. There are real consequences for rejecting wisdom, for scoffing at wisdom. If we scoff and laugh at God's wise divine proclamation, wisdom will laugh at us when calamity strikes. It doesn't mean God is laughing at you; Wisdom is laughing because she has been calling out and now it's too late. When your daughter is pregnant, when there's a drug addiction, when the marriage is really over you have waited too late to avoid the wreck that Wisdom would have warned you about. Wisdom says that when the calamity comes, it is just too late to benefit from my warning.

> Proverbs 1:28 -30
> 28 Then they will call upon me, but I will not answer;
> they will seek me diligently but will not find me.
> 29 Because they hated knowledge
> and did not choose the fear of the LORD,
> 30 would have none of my counsel
> and despised all my reproof…

If wisdom is calling out and you are not willing to listen, when the disaster comes why should wisdom answer? So Wisdom is just silent. Fear doesn't usually set in until a disaster happens. Then everyone begins to call on Wisdom, "Where are you? Wisdom, wisdom, where are you!?" But wisdom is silent then. If the gullible and the scoffer and the fool refused wisdom for so long, what good would it do now?

Take note of the real problem in 1:29:

> They hated knowledge and
> did not choose the fear of the Lord."

You should mark that in your Bible: "The beginning of wisdom is the fear of the Lord" (Proverbs 9:10). Wisdom brings knowledge and begins by fearing the Lord. Many blame God the minute something goes wrong. Now He may have been telling them to listen to wisdom all along, but the minute something goes wrong, it's all His fault. They will not accept wisdom's counsel and they despise her reproof—her course correction. And so what happens?

Proverbs 1:31
Therefore they shall eat the fruit of their way,
and have their fill of their own devices.

Those who reject the way of Wisdom will get their fill of their own way. That's what's happening in our country, in our churches and in many lives. The turning away from wisdom of the gullible will slay them. The prosperity, the financial material success of a fool who rejects God will wind up destroying him. But look again at what God desires for us:

Proverbs 1:33
But whoever listens to me will dwell secure
and will be at ease, without dread of disaster."

You don't have to be afraid. No fear of sudden destruction. You will live securely. It doesn't mean that it will be all smooth sailing, but it does mean that your boat will not be destroyed on the rocks. Your boat will not sink and you will not drown.

Wise Living

Statistics say there is a 60% divorce rate right now in 1993. That would indicate that two-thirds of my children will wind up divorced. But that is not necessarily so. I don't plan for any of my three children to be divorced. It may happen, but we don't *plan* on it working out that way. We're teaching them skill in how to live life from God's perspective; we are teaching them wisdom. It has to be taught pre-marital, during marriage and all along.

My wife and I are already practicing on being grandparents. We don't even have any yet, but I'm going to be an incredible granddaddy! I've told my three children that I've been praying for almost twenty four years that God would give each of them three children a piece just like mine. I want nine grandchildren. Then I'm not going to tell my children how to handle them! In fact, I'm going to tell my grandchildren how to bug my children—where to put the needle, how to irritate them—so my kids can grow up! I believe that's how God uses our children.

My definition of parenting is two consenting adults agreeing to commit gradual suicide. That's what parenting is, but it's a lot of fun. I'm looking forward to being a grandparent and personally enrolling all of my grandchildren in every sport, every activity to fill up all twelve months of the year, every morning and night, weekdays, weekends. I've already taught my children you need to be at every practice, every recital, every game. We are looking forward to paying back our kids for what they did to us! We're looking forward to that. My children don't want to have any children for some reason; I don't understand why.

If you look at today's statistics they only tell us that we have a lot of novice sailors. The divorce rate, the single parent families, broken homes, drug addiction, alcoholism—none of those people *planned* for any of that. Nobody has ever set out saying, "I'd like to destroy my life," but it happens.

The secret is to know that as the winds start to blow, and the tides of culture begin to take us out to sea and the rocks are there, as grandparents and as a parents, we can learn how to sail into the wind. You know why? Because God made the wind. If you just know the God who made the wind and listen to His wisdom you can learn.

I believe that deep down we all want to be wise parents. We all want to be good mates for our spouses. None of us ever set out to have our life wreck on the rocks or capsize or simply drift aimlessly out at sea, losing a lot of time. None of us plan that and yet it happens.

We have to balance these forces that are pushing against us in life; It's our responsibility. The best sailing teacher I know is the one who authored every word of this Bible: the Holy Spirit. Jesus says,

> He (the Holy Spirit) will glorify me, for he will take what is mine and declare it to you.   John 16:14

God delights to teach his children. In the last of his life, John said,

> I have no greater joy than to hear that my children are walking in the Truth.   3 John 1:4

You can learn wisdom. You can learn to walk in the Truth. All you have to do is ask God and then get in His Word.

Prayer

Father we thank you that your truth sets us free from ignorance and the powerful forces that are blowing against us in the world. We thank you that wisdom is still crying in the streets. She is still walking in the public places and again and again she keeps reproving us. Teach us not to despise her reproof. We don't like to be shown that we're wrong, that maybe we don't know, that maybe we need to come to You and sit at Your feet and cry out for skill in living. We know there are bright prospects for those who are sitting at Your feet, the One who made all the winds. Father, we ask you to teach us how to sail into the winds so that we can pass that wisdom on to others. In Christ's name, Amen.

CHAPTER 6

The Point of Action

"When the man saw that he could not defeat Jacob, he struck the socket of his hip so that it was dislocated while he wrestled with him. Then the man said, "Let me go, for the dawn is breaking." "I will not let you go," Jacob replied, "unless you bless me."
GENESIS 32:25–26

In Genesis 27, we find the beginning of the story of Jacob. You'll remember Jacob, he was a manipulator and a deceiver. If you look that Hebrew name "Jacob" up, you will discover that it means something like, cheater, liar, thief, supplanter, deceiver, manipulator. Jacob's name fit his personality. Jacob was his mother Rebekah's favorite and she protected him, ran interference for him and taught him how to work his father and brother. You remember that Jacob manipulated his brother Esau out of his birthright and deceived his father Isaac so that he would give him the birthright. Once Esau figured out what had happened, he decided to kill Jacob.

Rebekah told Jacob to run to his uncle Laban's house. Along the way, he had a vision and God revealed himself to Jacob, telling him that He would be with him and bless him and fulfill the promises given to his grandfather Abraham through Him (see Genesis 28:10-

17). As Jacob woke up from the vision, he realized something incredible had happened. I want to pick up the story right there:

> Genesis 28:16–17
> "Then Jacob woke up and thought, "Surely the LORD is in this place, but I did not realize it!" He was afraid and said, "What an awesome place this is! This is nothing else than the house of God! This is the gate of heaven!"

Jacob had an encounter with God. You might call this Jacob's "conversion experience." He took the stones that he had set out for his pillows and made a pillar. Then he poured oil on top of it and he called the name of that place Bethel, which means "House of God." Now listen to what Jacob says:

> Genesis 28:20–22
> "Then Jacob made a vow, saying, "If God will be with me and will keep me in this way that I go, and will give me bread to eat and clothing to wear, so that I come again to my father's house in peace, then the LORD shall be my God, and this stone, which I have set up for a pillar, shall be God's house. And of all that you give me I will give a full tenth to you."

Did you notice all the "ifs" in that? "*If* God gives me this and *if* He does that … then the Lord will be my God." Then he ends the vow saying *if* God will do all of this, then I will give Him a tenth. Isn't that nice of Jacob?

Now you may remember that Jacob went over to Laban's house and wound up working seven years in order to get beautiful Rachel for a wife. But Laban was as deceptive as Jacob and he tricked him and gave him the less attractive Leah in disguise. Jacob was manipulator but he ran into a more skilled manipulator and he lost that contest. Now Jacob worked another 7 years in order to get Rachel, the wife he wanted in the first place. If you follow those stories in Genesis 29-32 you find out that Jacob was conniving all the time and by the end he has Laban wanting to kill him as well.

By the time we get to the middle of Genesis 32, we have come forward twenty years since Jacob met God at Bethel. Esau is back on Jacob's trail, and it looks like he is coming to kill him. God appears again to Jacob and an interesting thing happens. We will pick up the story there:

> Now Jacob was left alone. Then a man wrestled with him until daybreak. When the man saw that he could not defeat Jacob, he struck the socket of his hip so the socket of Jacob's hip was dislocated while he wrestled with him.
>
> Then the man said, "Let me go, for the dawn is breaking."
> "I will not let you go," Jacob replied, "unless you bless me."
> The man asked him, "What is your name?"
> He answered, "Jacob."
> "No longer will your name be Jacob," the man told him, "but Israel, because you have fought with God and with men and have prevailed."
> Then Jacob asked, "Please tell me your name."
> "Why do you ask my name?" the man replied. Then he blessed Jacob there.
> So Jacob named the place Peniel, explaining, "Certainly I have seen God face to face and have survived."
> The sun rose over him as he crossed over Penuel, but he was limping because of his hip." Genesis 32:24–31

Jacob wrestled with God all night long! In fact, God always wrestles with men. That's why boys fight all the time. It's the way God made us. The way a boy establishes his masculinity is through showing his power; he has to wrestle, he has to fight. That's the way God deals with a man. He wrestles. He's wrestling with every man in some way—in different ways, but He wrestles.

The ladies stand back and say, "Why are you so hard headed? Why don't you just give in?" Not that you ladies don't have wrestling matches with God too. But men are tenaciously hard headed. It's in the wrestling with God that He bends us to His will. Jacob wrestled with God all night—he wouldn't yield.

But then the Lord touched Jacob's thigh and put an end to the fight. Jacob still clung to Him and would not let Him go until the Lord blessed him. At that point, the Lord asks, "What is your name?" Jacob tells him his name: "I am Jacob" (the deceiver, the supplanter, the manipulator). I think here Jacob is owning up to his name. For the past twenty years he has been a deceiver and manipulator. Jacob has reached what I am going to call his point of action: *he has been beaten down to the point where he is ready for something to change.*

It took God 20 years to get Jacob to be honest. And now that Jacob has owned up to his name, the Lord gives him another one: "You will now be called *Israel,* for you have fought with God and men and have prevailed." That is what the name "Israel" means—"the one who fights or wrestles with God." If you look there in Genesis 32:29-30 Jacob is convinced that this "man" or "messenger" that he has been fighting with is the Lord God Himself! As the story closes, Jacob is moving on, limping away.

Now that is a long introduction but I wanted you to hear it because it touches on all the points that I would like to cover with you. We are going to be talking about *your point of action.* What is a point of action? The point of action is that point in time when you will do something. When will you do something? Not until the pain moves you to action. It is what this chart represents:

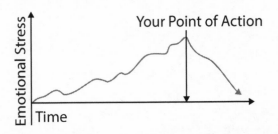

Now this is a sad truth, but we generally won't act until pressure becomes painful for us. It's just human nature. You can have something that's bothering you and you won't go to the dentist or the doctor as long as it's just low pressure, something you can tolerate. But If you get a full blown toothache at 3:00 in the morning, you don't care who you disturb or who has to get out of bed. You don't care who's inconvenienced; you just need relief and you want it now. That's the point of action. It's not very smart but it's very normal.

Finding The Point of Action

Some of you have raised children or are raising children. What we discover is our children are masters at using your point of action. They know that as the day progresses and your emotions get spent you are moving closer and closer to that point you'll do something. When I was a kid growing up I knew when my mother called out my whole name, "Tom Murray!" she had reached her point of action. When she called out all three of my names—"John Thomas Murray!"—I knew she had *really* reached her point of action.

Your child is a student of you as a parent. They know how far they can take you before you will do anything. It's the fifth time you say, "If you do that again. Now, I'm not telling you again, do you understand me?" They have our number. They understand where our point of action is and they know how far we will go before we reach that point of action.

We all learn where this point of action is with everyone we are in a relationship with. If you are a husband and you are in a heated "discussion" with your wife and she begins to cry, you lose. If you are a boss, all your employees know where your point of action is. They have figured out how much they have to do before you will get on them. If we watch and study, we can find out where anyone's point of action is.

Now we know that God Himself is the ideal parent. He knows what He is doing. As Christians we are His children and at some point we want to figure out where His point of action is. "How far can I go before God will get me? How far can I take God?" That is a question we have all thought about before.

Moving the Point of Action Back

Here is the problem with this way of doing things: we wind up living with a lot of stress and emotional turmoil in our relationships. But we don't have to live this way. I want to share some ways you can move your point of action back earlier in this whole time frame so that you don't have to enter into all the stress.

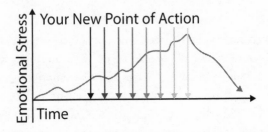

It's a lot easier to deal with your kids over on the left side of your chart than it is when you are over on the right all stressed and frazzled. You don't have to go through that. Your children, your husband, your wife, your employer—whoever it may be—are going to play by the rules you set in this "game." You set the rules by the way you engage in the conversation. Let me share a couple of points with you.

Make Reasonable Expectations. The first thing to keep in mind is that you have to be reasonable. With your kids the burden is on you to ask, "Is what I am saying and doing fair?" Our children were never allowed to climb on the coffee tables and swing from the light fixtures. This is a *fair* and *reasonable* expectation that we can all agree on. Since we can all agree on that, we can move on. We tried to have as few rules as possible. So the whole "keep it simple stupid" really applies here.

Give Clear Instruction. The second thing you have do is give clear instruction. Be sure you're reasonable, but also be sure you're clear. If my children had trashed the den and we decided that was unacceptable we made that clear to them as an expectation for the family. The den wasn't going to be a museum, but the den wasn't going to be a disaster zone either.

Consistently Apply Your Expectations. It didn't matter if we were the only ones in our house or if we had company, our children were never allowed to dance on the coffee tables or swing from the lights. So our fair expectations and rules are also consistently applied. Consistency is essential to this whole process.

Something you younger parents need to know is that your children will test your consistent application of your rules. Children have this incredible ability to know when you are vulnerable. They can be *emotional terrorists*! If you don't apply expectations consistently, you kids will learn how to push you to your limits quickly.

If you want to see kids bully mothers, go to the supermarket. I like to go with Jeannie and just stand back and observe what is going on. Kids are bringing things and throwing them in the baskets. Mothers are haggled and frayed. They're trying to negotiate, but you can never negotiate with a terrorist!

We all want our kids to look like little angels even when they're really not. It's amazing, all the dog and pony shows I've watched as parents try to control their children and look good in front of friends and other church members. But then, we they get into the car all the death threats begin, "If you ever treat me that way again … !"

If you are a man, let me give you a piece of advice: never try to negotiate with a woman or a child; you'll lose every time. Whenever Jeannie and I have something to discuss, I never look at her eyes because I can't think. That's why she's always trying to make eye contact with me. She'll say, "Will you look at me!" and I'll say, "I can't. If I look at you I can't think." It's like a snake charming a bird out of a tree. Their eyes dance and they can do all these crazy things to your head. I'm easy to deal with but when my wife or my kids start talking, everything I say seems stupid. Everything, every reason I give is totally illogical. If you ever get into a sheer logic discussion with your wife, you are going to loose.

We have tried to make our expectations fair, clear and consistent. This sets up some boundaries so that we don't get pushed to our maximum stress level.

Get Feedback. Once you've communicated, you don't know if there has been a reception on the other end. I define communication as the meeting of meaning. You always have to ask the last question, "Did you hear and understand me?" You want to make sure that you have engaged the mind.

If you ask that question and they say, "Excuse me, what were you saying?," you can know that you didn't connect. If you say to one of your kids, "At the next commercial break, will you take your stuff to you room please," and they don't give any feedback, you can guess what is probably going to happen: nothing. You can get mad but they still probably won't understand what you're mad about because they didn't hear what you said.

My wife constantly says that I'm in the twilight zone. I can be completely looking straight at you, but my mind is in outer space. Then I will hear out of the corner of my ear, "I'm planning to kill myself tonight and I thought I'd just let you know."

"Were you talking to me?" I say…

I know that just because you've given a fair, clear instruction doesn't mean you've communicated.

This is like a game. One person makes a move and the other person has to counter. You have to ask the question, "Did you understand me?" You may have to stand in front of the TV, get face to face, mano-e-mano to get their attention in order to communicate clearly. But until you are sure they have heard you and acknowledged that they understand you expectations and requests, you cannot expect them to act. You have to make sure that you have engaged their mind.

Now you have to engage the will. You have to ask, "Can we work together on this?" For you kids you have to ask, "Are you going to obey me?" Now you're appealing to the will. You make sure they get the message, but it is going to be up to them what they do about it.

Moving the Point of Action Back
with Your Children

As a parent, you can set your point of action wherever you want it along your chart. Your children will learn to work within those parameters. Once your kids know where your point of action is, they will work according to it. You can actually move the point of action back so that your child will act the first time you tell them something.

There's only one reason why anybody does anything they do: because it works. If your children have learned that you are not going to get serious about things until you have reached your point of maximum stress, they are going to use that to their advantage. There is enough stress in life and we should have to live distressed by the way we are manipulating in our relationships. You don't have to live like that, as a parent or as a Christian.

How do you stop that? You just don't let it work. You have to decide that you are going to move that point back and clearly communicate to them according to all that we have just discussed. When they test you on it, you tell them, "Time out; that was a nice try but that is not going to work anymore." It will take patience and consistency on your part, but you can move their point of action back so that when you speak, they respond.

You may think that I am being unrealistic, but I can tell you it will work. You will have to compete with MTV or Nickelodeon, or whatever else is distracting them. At first you have to be very creative. But you can start using their own tactics against them. Our children usually don't have any trouble getting our attention. If you're trying to carry on a conversation with another adult, they will start to dance around you, tugging at you. They'll do whatever they have to do until finally respond. You may have to do the same types of things to get their attention—get on your knees and get face to face, eye to eye. Eventually, if you are as persistent as they are, you will see progress.

The Point of Action with Your Heavenly Father

"Does the LORD take pleasure in burnt offerings and
sacrifices as much as he does in obeying His voice?
Certainly, obedience is better than sacrifice;
paying attention is better than the fat of rams.
                                                    1 Samuel 15:22

You have a Heavenly Father. He would like a relationship where He could speak to you and you would be immediately ready to do as He asks. Instead of saying, "God do I have to? How long can I wait?"

As Fathers, it is important that we train our children to respond quickly. If you let them drag you into your time of maximum stress, you're actually cheating your child. You see if you let your children run all over you as an earthly Father, they will think they can do the same thing with their Heavenly Father.

As Fathers, we affect our children's understanding of their Heavenly Father. When a child thinks about the Heavenly Father, he relates it to his earthly father. As a father, are you fair? Are you consistent? Are you clear? Our Heavenly Father is and we should represent that to our children. The sooner you can train them to respond quickly, the better off things will be for everyone.

So the main question that we have to end on is, "*How far does your Heavenly Father have to move you until you reach your point of action?*" If you are a mature Christian, or want to be a mature Christian, that is measured by how quickly you move in your relationship to God. How many times does He have to say something? To what extent does He have to go to pound it into your head? The sign of a mature child is the Father speaks and we act. That's what God is looking for.

The question becomes, "How far are you trying to push God?" Many Christians are "Jacobs" wrestling with God. The "Israels" say, "The Lord said it, I'll do it." Are you asking God, "How far do I have to go before you will do what is necessary?"

People will ask me, "How can I know where the Father is trying to move my point of action back?" I can tell you: all you have to do is ask. Just close your eyes and ask and the Holy Spirit will tell you. You just have to ask, "What am I being rebellious about?" You don't need to go and sit in a confession booth and try to pour your heart out. Just ask the Holy Spirit. Jesus said He will guide you in all truth.

Are you resisting your Heavenly Father's efforts to parent you? If you are saying, "I'm not going to do that unless you bring enough pain into my life … " let me just warn you, He will. Our Heavenly Father is the perfect Father and He will do whatever it takes to shape us into His glorious children. I have pushed against Him and resisted and He has lovingly reduced me to child who simply comes wanting to climb up in His arms and say, "I'm sorry."

He can move me to my point of action when others can't. He can do it when my pastor can't. He can do it when my family can't. He can do it when all my friends can't. God is the ideal parent. He knows how to get you and me to come with tears in our eyes, a brokenness in our heart, knowing that His goal was not to hurt us but to mature us. He will do whatever He has to do to get you to hear and obey.

God uses all the principles that we have discussed in our relationship with Him. In His Written Word, He tells us what He wants; He clearly states His expectations. Then He says, "My child, did you understand me?" You acknowledge by believing and trusting what He has said. The next thing He says is, "Are you going to obey me?" If you ignore Him, or refuse to obey once you have clearly understood Him, He will bring you to your knees—not out of punishment, but out of love. He wants to move our point of action back so that we are freed from our slavery to sin.

Our Heavenly Father desires a relationship with us where as soon as He speaks, we act. That's maturity. In the passage above, Samuel said, "Listen, to obey is better than anything you can do in the eyes of God." God is reasonable. He is consistent. He always has your best interest at heart. But he will bring as much pain as is necessary to bring you to a teachable moment, to bring you to a point of action.

I've looked back at my pilgrimage as a child of God and I see He has allowed me to do this and do that, maybe taking years to run the loop just like Jacob. Finally, in one of those cataclysmic moments, He reduces me to get my attention: "Son, do you understand what this whole exercise is about?"

I would say, "Yes Sir."

"Do you understand? Are you tired, worn out, ready to yield?"

The minute I yield, He reminds me, "You'll be a prince with God, no longer a manipulator." The greatest manipulation going on in life today isn't between children and parents, it's between God's children and Him. We want to know how far we can take our Heavenly Father when we ought to be asking, "How quickly will I obey?"

Prayer

Father we thank you for the truth that you are a perfect Heavenly Father. We thank you for your truth that sets us free from the stress and turmoil of manipulation and rebellion. We thank you that you love us, your children, with an unconditional love and that you will also discipline us for our good, that we may share in your holiness. I pray for all those who have been wrestling with you, maybe for years, that they would give in and receiving the blessing of peace that comes from hearing your word and obeying your voice. In Christ's name, Amen.

CHAPTER 7

Cleaning Old Wells

"Drink water from your own cistern,
flowing water from your own well."
PROVERBS 5:15

Are you aware that over 50% of all the marriages in America today end in divorce? I've often wondered about the 50% that do survive, how many of them are really happy? How many of them are really fulfilled? How many of them, if they were really honest, have found their expectations met in their marriage? I am not sure that all the survivors are happy; some of them are just that, survivors. I had a man tell me once that, "A man isn't complete until he is married and then he's finished!" If you think about that for a minute, that is a fairly pessimistic view of marriage and fulfillment.

As you think about the 50% that are failing today, do you think they went to the altar planning to fail? Do you think they went with the idea that marriage is like Kleenex tissues—they're disposable. If it doesn't work out, you just toss this one and get another one. I have talked with a lot of people and that hasn't been my experience. Most want to be married and fulfilled in that relationship.

I'm counseling a couple right now—we'll call them Dickey and Joy—who are about to get married. They grew up in our high school and collegiate Bible studies. I have asked them, "Going into marriage, what is your greatest fear?" They have both said, "We are afraid that our marriage will fail and we don't want to wind up in that 50%." They see their friends who are married, who dated and said all the right things and seemed to be in love, but are now biting and cutting one another, fighting like cats and dogs.

Dickey and Joy are in love but they are terrified. Dickey is absolutely terrified that their marriage will fail. As they look at the reality of their friend's marriages, they have said to me, "It makes us wonder if we should even try it."

So they ask me, "Can you tell us that we will have permanency in our marriage?"

"So you want your marriage to be healthy?"

"Oh yes. We don't want it to get sick."

"Do you want it to grow?" I ask.

"Oh yeah we want it to grow."

"Do you want it to be permanent?"

"Oh yeah. We want this to last until death do us part. We're not saying idle vows. We want to be in that 50% that survives."

Now I have encouraged them not only to be in the 50% that survives but to become part of that much smaller percentage who are actually fulfilled. So what does it take to make a marriage relationship be all it can be?

We are going to touch on a very unpopular topic—commitment. However, if we want not only to survive but to find fulfillment in our relationships commitment is necessary, especially our marriage. I want you to understand that *without commitment there is no fulfillment.*

The Necessity of Mutual Commitment

The foundation of any relationship is mutual commitment. Whether we are talking about marriage, parent to child, employee to employer, friend to friend, mutual commitment is essential to having fulfillment, growth, health, and permanency in any relationship. One person can't do all the committing. It takes two people to have a relationship, so it has to be mutual. *Without mutual commitment there is no fulfillment.*

God is just as committed to that principle as He is to the law of gravity. If you are not committed to be somebody's friend, you'll never be satisfied as a friend. If you are not committed in your career, you will never find career fulfillment. If you are not committed to God, you will never be spiritually fulfilled. If you are not committed to your spouse, you will never find fulfillment in marriage. If you are not committed as a parent to your child, you will never find fulfillment as a parent. It just won't happen.

So we if understand that mutual commitment is necessary, we then need to talk about the nature of this mutual commitment. Let me give you four trigger words that will outline the four ingredients of mutual commitment. The type of commitment I will be talking about is Exclusive, Exhaustive, Expensive and Extensive.

Now think about those four ideas in the context of marriage vows. When I said, "I, Tom, take you Jeannie to be my lawfully wedded wife, forsaking all others …" I was making an exclusive commitment. Now I am "out of the market." Because of the commitment, I can't go around looking for another model, or a "newer model." I have taken my wife "for better or worse."

That commitment is also exhaustive, "forsaking all others … till death do us part." That pretty much covers all of my life from that point forward. It's also expensive, "for richer or for poorer,"—it is going to take everything I have to make this work. Whatever it costs me, I will do it. And finally, those vows are extensive, "in sickness and in health, in good times and in bad times."

Commitment is Exclusive
In Proverbs, we are called to make our commitment exclusive:

> "15 Drink water from your own cistern
>   and running water from your own well.
> 5:16 Should your springs be dispersed outside,
>   your streams of water in the wide plazas?

5:17 Let them be for yourself alone,
      and not for strangers with you." Proverbs 5:15-17

This is talking about marital exclusiveness, comparing the marriage to a well and the water it produces. Drink from your own well and just let it be yours. We are going to come back to this with the next couple of verses. As Solomon will go on to explain, fulfillment is found in giving yourself to one person.

Commitment is Exhaustive

In the Song of Solomon 2:16, the young bride says: "My beloved is mine and I am his." That's exhaustive. My husband belongs to me and I belong to him. Later in Chapter 7:10, the lover says "I am my beloved's and his desire is toward me." His total desire is toward me. There is something binding about two people saying, "I'm yours and you're mine. I mean that exhaustively, with everything that's in me." Exhaustive also means that this is a life-long commitment, "till death do us part."

A lot of people that come to see me are really only interested in a wedding not a marriage. They come and say, "Will you marry us?" I say, "Well, may I ask you a question? What do you mean by that? What have you got in mind?"

As they talk, I often realize they haven't got a clue to what marriage really involves. I explain the nature of commitment to them. Then I ask them, "Are you willing to make this kind of commitment and not just show up at the church for a ceremony? Are you then willing to nurture this commitment throughout your marriage?"

An exhaustive, exclusive commitment will produce very stable people. This will produce very stable marriages. When we understand this, that our commitments are exhaustive and exclusive, and this is more than just words we say, then we are going to have stable families. If you have stable families you are going to have a stable society and nation. Because people don't want to commit, we have instability in our families, instability in our society, and instability in our leadership, instability in individuals and even in the body of Christ.

But when you have an exclusive, exhaustive commitment, we are only a part of the way there.

Commitment is Expensive

As I have counseled Dickey, I told him that when we get to the altar I'm going to ask him a question that we are going to have to work on before we get there. Now it would be easy if I just asked Dickey if he loved Joy. I'm sure he would very easily say, "Oh yeah, no question!" The Bible, however, raises the bar for a husband. The more crucial question that I am asking Dickey is, "Will you love this woman as Christ loved the church?"

That is a harder question. I have explained to Dickey all that is involved in loving Joy the way Christ loved the church. There isn't any expense that Christ would spare for His bride, the Church. His love cost Him everything, even His life. Jesus didn't just get in it for the short haul either. He has committed Himself fully to us until the day He gets us home. He loves us when we're not loveable. He's patient and kind and long suffering. He has committed exclusively to us. He is the bridegroom and we are the bride.

There's nobody in the whole universe that's busier than Christ. The Bible says that He sustains the whole universe by the word of His power (Hebrews 1:3). But He's never too busy for the bride. He's the high priest of every believer on the earth. He's listening to the prayers of all His people, all over the world. He'll always drop whatever He is doing to talk to us the minute we need Him.

So I said to Dickey, "I want you to commit to love Joy in the way that Christ loves His Bride. That is what we are called to—not the world's standards, but Christ's standards. You need to count that cost and understand what this will take." I sent Dickey home numb to think about that, but at least he knows the truth. His fiancé Joy said, "Amen!" to all of this. I said, "Joy, we haven't even gotten to your part honey!"

Commitment is Extensive

Let's keep on reading in Proverbs:

> 18 Let your fountain be blessed,
>   and rejoice in the wife of your youth,
>   19 a lovely deer, a graceful doe.
> Let her breasts fill you at all times with delight;
>   be intoxicated always in her love.
> 20 Why should you be intoxicated, my son,
>   with a forbidden woman
>   and embrace the bosom of an adulteress?
> 21 For a man's ways are before the eyes of the LORD,
>   and he ponders all his paths.   Proverbs 5:18–21

"Let your fountain be blessed and rejoice with the wife of your youth"—That is the wife that you started with! And notice it doesn't say endure, It says rejoice! That is the goal to rejoice with your wife. You don't want to just say, "We made it. We lasted. We beat the odds." You should be able to say, "Listen, we committed, we've nurtured, and we didn't just survive; our marriage is greater now than it ever has been!"

In verse 19 Solomon compares a wife to a deer, a doe. Large gentle eyes, long soft ears, slender legs, that's what a deer is—graceful and beautiful. Solomon said let your wife be that to you. "Let her breasts satisfy you at all times and be intoxicated with her love," he says.

The Bible has a lot to say about sexuality. People tend to think God is embarrassed about those topics. God isn't the least bit embarrassed—He designed and engineered all of it. Not only did He give us the equipment, He gave us the appetite. Where we get in trouble is when we take the equipment and appetite He gave us and try to find satisfaction without His wisdom.

When God created all things, at each step He said, "This is good." The first time God said, "It is not good" was when he said, "It is not good for the man to be alone." You will remember that God brought all the animals before Adam for him to name. That was probably the best Sex-Ed class ever held! Can you imagine Adam seeing the males giving their mating call and the females answering? It probably didn't take long for Adam to figure out there was no female counterpart to answer his mating call! I have wondered if God did that to educate Adam and also to stir up his appetite. I think God wanted Adam to understand that He would satisfy any appetite that He had given him.

So God put Adam to sleep and made Eve. When Adam looked up and he saw Eve, he said, "Wow! She is at least a 10." I don't imagine God had to explain much to Adam about the way things worked. God had created the equipment and the appetite and now He had provided a way for fulfillment. Adam was intoxicated with Eve.

So Solomon says, "Go ahead and enjoy what God has provided— be intoxicated with your wife." When we really get into the meaning of marriage and what God had in mind, He intended for the man and the woman to come together in a relationship not only to share all their mental and emotional selves but also their physical bodies. There is a marvelous, deep, fulfillment for any man and woman who's prepared to mutually commit to one another on God's terms.

Solomon also asks a question that gives a warning, "Why would you be intoxicated by a strange woman—an adulteress?" There's no fulfillment in that. Where there's no commitment there is no fulfillment. God Himself watches and says, "I don't understand. They tell me they want fulfillment but then they won't listen to my wisdom, my truth." The Lord is watching all that we do and pondering our ways.

Digging and Maintaining Wells

I want you to take note of something we just read in Proverbs 5:15, "Drink water from your own cistern and running water from your own well." Proverbs talks about cisterns, wells, fountains and rivers as metaphors. The most important ingredient in sustaining life is water. That is true anywhere you go. If you don't have water, you're in a desert. In the context of the Ancient Middle East, wells and cisterns were the place you would go to find water.

Wells didn't just appear out in the middle of the desert. A well was the result of a lot of work. It was very costly to dig a well but the minute the well was completed, it became the focal point of all community life. Villages and settlements were built around wells, because the water they contained meant life.

Let's talk just a minute about one of the ways wells were dug in ancient times. Out in the sandy parts of the Middle East, they couldn't go out and start digging a well straight down because the sand would cave in on them. So they would start way back from the point the well would be and dig a series of steps downs in the sand. Sometimes they would have to start a hundred yards out. Sometimes they would dig in a couple of directions, both moving toward the center of the well. When they got down far enough, they would hit the water table and the well would begin to fill.

Now think about all that sand that was getting excavated. They would have to move it all to another place by hand. I think you are beginning to realize how much labor it took. Someone had to commit to the hard labor of digging the well. Once they committed, they had to go to work.

Solomon talks about another way they would get water in mountainous regions where there was more rock. In the mountains they would get some water from winter snowfall and seasonal rains but it would all run off. They didn't have any water for the rest of the year. So they would go out find a good location and chisel a cistern to collect the water in the rock. You can imagine how much labor it took, down on your knees chiseling away.

When Solomon uses these metaphors of wells and cisterns in his proverbs, he is telling us that relationships are essential to life. They are as essential as water to a man in the desert.

Digging a well or carving out a cistern is just the first part; now you have to maintain it. When a new well was dug, I am sure everyone was excited and would go down and drink the crystal clear, sparkling, cool water. But in the desert, the winds blow all the time. They're blowing tumble weeds, trash, and debris. So while you were sleeping or at work, trash was blowing into the well all the time.

To maintain the well meant that every day you had to go and see what kind of shape the well was in. You might have to shore up the wall of the well or clean trash out. You know what happens to the water when you neglect the well? It begins to get polluted, putrid, and sour. During the night, animals that are sick and dying might come across the desert looking for water and stumble down the steps and get in the well. Some would die right in the well. What would happen if no one cleaned out that well? It would quickly get to where nobody wanted to drink from it, let alone even be around it.

Doesn't that sound like some marriages? I don't know many people that didn't enjoy their honeymoon and the few days right after, and maybe the weeks or a month or two after. But then they start to lose commitment to the maintenance and the trash starts to pile in. The wife says, "That's your trash." The husband says, "That's not mine; that's yours!" Pretty soon, no one is taking care of the well. Before long the marriage gets polluted and sour. All you have to do to let a well get polluted is just ignore it.

Let me tell one important truth about old wells: The water is still sweet it's just under all the garbage. The same water that you loved many years ago it's still down there, just as clear, crystal and pristine, just as satisfying as it was the day you got married. It's just all choked up with the goop and the junk and the debris.

As I have counseled Dickey and Joy, I have asked them, "Are you prepared every morning to say to each other, "I'm really concerned for the well being of our well today. What can we do together to make sure there's no trash in the well?" I know they both want the water to be as sweet five years from now, as it is today. The only way I know to do that is to maintain the well by cleaning the trash out. This has to be a mutual commitment. It can't be a 60/40 split. Everyday, they both have to give 100% to maintaining the well.

Now think about the cistern for a minute. In the desert there are shifts and little earthquakes. No matter how well you chiseled out the granite, when the earth shifted, the rock would sheer and crack. So how was that maintained? You would have to seal all the cracks. They patched them every day. If you don't patch the cracks, the water will leak out.

If marriage is like a well or a cistern, you have to have two people mutually committed to dig the well and then to maintain it. We are going to keep the pollutants out and we are going to patch all the cracks. How often? Daily. This has to be done everyday. How long do you want the water to be sweet? Every day. How often do you have to clean the well? Every day.

That's how you dig and maintain a well and take care of an older one. You know what people tend to want to do with old wells? Go dig another one. They want to punt the old one that reeks and go dig a new one.

If you read the story of Isaac, the first thing he had to do when he went back to the land was to clean out the old wells (see Genesis 26:18). The wells had fallen into a state of disrepair. They'd been neglected. Nobody wanted to drink from those wells because they had become putrid.

But Isaac said, "This well was good enough for our forefathers. It's good enough for us." So he and all his family cleaned the old wells to get down to the good water. The problem wasn't the well; the problem was the maintenance program. He cleaned the old wells.

From Survival to Fulfillment

When a couple comes to me for premarital counseling and they don't want to be part of the statistical failures and they don't want to be part of the survivors who only survive, I want them for them too. But I also want them to count the cost and understand the truth about what that is going to take. So before they say, "I do," I talk about this proverb and the digging of wells.

A couple who counts the cost and genuinely says, "We are willing to commit exhaustively, exclusively and we are willing to spare no expense and to go as long as it takes," is a couple that is set up to last. Not only will they be set to succeed but they will raise some very healthy children who will "rise up and call them blessed" (Proverbs 31:28). They are likely to be some very happy grandparents one day.

When I was 27 and got married to my wife. I said, "I do," and I meant it. I didn't understand what that really meant but I did mean it as much as you can mean it at 27. It has taken me 26 years to find out what "I do" really means. You can say those words in a moment but it takes a lifetime to realize their significance. I am committed not only to the maintenance of the well but also to the wellbeing of the well. I do want my children to say, "Yes I'd like to have a marriage like yours." I want my daughter to say, "Dad I'd like to find someone like you," and for my son to say "Mom, how can I find someone like you?" No marriage is going to be perfect but it can be fulfilling if you have two people who are in that well all the time, cleaning, working, patching—talking and resolving things.

I had three buddies—we were called the four musketeers—and we all ran around together for years. Within six months, all three of my friends got married and within six months all three of my friends were running around on their wives. I became a confirmed bachelor. I said,

"That is not from me." I came from a broken home and I wasn't going to have one.

Then I met Jeannie. I dated Jeannie for three and one-half years and never once said, "I love you"—not for three and a half years! She told me she loved me; she couldn't help it. She asked me one time, "Don't you love me?" I said, "Jeannie the day I tell you I love you is the day I'll ask you to marry me and I will mean it."

Finally, her sister told her, "He's a loser; three and a half years is enough." At that point she was teaching school and she was asked by one of her friends to go to Europe, to France, for the summer. She came to me and asked me what I thought about it. Well, benevolent me, I said "Well, you're single—when else are you ever going to get to go? You ought to go." Now what I didn't know is that was her way of trying to get me to say, "Oh don't go; I'd be lost without you." The minute I told her to go, boy she got hot. She decided she had to go and go she did.

She borrowed all the money out of the teacher's credit union that they'd lend her. She bought clothes at places I'd never even heard of. Do any of you remember The Snooty Fox? I didn't know there was one, let alone a snooty one. She even bought a brand new '65 Mustang.

She hadn't been gone on the "SS France" more than two days before I was writing her letters. I'd never written her letters but I was sick; I missed her. You know what I was thinking: "She's gonna get over there in Europe and somebody's gonna make a move on my girl!" Suddenly, I wasn't so secure. Every place in Europe she went there was a letter waiting from me—every single stop at every hotel.

Now when she finally came home, I picked her up and said "I love you. I want to marry you." But she didn't believe me. She went home and decided to lay low. The next morning, my mother called and said, "How are you, daughter-in-law?" Jeannie knew then that if I'd told my mom, I must be serious.

I will never forget seeing her dad when I asked for her hand. He really didn't care much for me then and he wasn't going to make it easy for me at all. I drove up and Jeannie walked out to the car and took me by the arm and grinned. We walked up to the front porch where her parents were rocking in rocking chairs. He looked at me and her mother grinned with that motherly look.

"I guess Jeannie told you about our talk," I said.

He said, "Yeah."

"Well did she tell you I asked her to marry me?"

He said, "Yes she told me."

"Well, I guess I'm asking you, is it alright if I marry her?"

He said, "Well do you love her?"

"Well, I think so."

"Think! Son, if you don't know by now, don't be asking me."

Then I said, "Yes sir I do, I do love her."

When I went down the aisle to make a commitment, I told Jeannie that my marriage wasn't going to be like my dad and mom's marriage. My marriage was not going to be like my friends' marriages. I didn't have a clue at that time how to nurture a marriage. I just knew what I didn't want. But I became very teachable. I said to God,

"Whatever it takes. I don't care what the expense. I don't care how long it takes. I don't care how exhaustive it is. I'll do it."

My wife and I had an agreement that we would never go to sleep with any cracks in our well. Now, we've laid back to back until 2 or 3 in the morning many, many times. There are times when I could just feel the steam rising from her. Finally we'd just get so sleepy one of us would turn and say, "Look, we have got to settle this. I have got to get some sleep." I am here to tell you, 26 years later, I haven't regretted a moment that we have spent cleaning our well and the water is still sweet. It's even sweeter in some respects because I know her better than I've ever known her at any time of my life.

I'd like to end by having you look one more time at Proverbs 5:15:

> Drink water from your own cistern,
>> flowing water from your own well.

Your marriage is a well that belongs to you. You have to work on it but also enjoy the water. Drink that water Solomon says. Let those flowing waters fulfill you, satisfy you. Can you see the waters of a pure well gushing, bubbling, and flowing? He says drink it, make it your own, enjoy it, satisfy all of your hunger—sexually, mentally, emotionally, and spiritually.

Finally he says, "Should your fountains be dispersed abroad, rivers of waters in the street." Do you know what that means? What you have with your spouse is not for others. God doesn't intend that. It's just for you. If you commit and you nurture your well, you will find that as years pass by it will remain clear and fresh. You will rejoice—not just exist and not just endure. You will actually rejoice with the wife of your youth.

I want to ask you one other question. If you are a Christian that means you are a bride of Christ. He committed. He's willing to maintain. I just want to ask you as we pray, what's the water like with your well with Christ? Is it sweet? As sweet as it was when you became a Christian? Is it sweeter? Or is all trashed up? If it has become polluted, He's willing to go to work. He's the faithful bridegroom but it has to be a mutual commitment. You have to go in the well together. Your well with Christ can be everything that it could ever be if you'll just get in the well and keep it maintained. Whether it is with our spouse or with Christ, the water of the well is as sweet as it ever was, it just may be hidden below the trash.

Prayer

Father, I thank you for reminding us that fulfillment in life is as essential as water in a desert. We thank you for your truth that sets us free to find true fulfilment in our relationships, especially in our marriages. We thank you that even if the well of our marriage has become polluted, there is still sweet water below the surface. Isaac cleaned old wells and he found that beneath all the pollution, beneath all the corruption, beneath all the junk, there was the bubbling water. I pray that we will be challenged as the bride of Christ to be sure that our heavenly marriage is healthy, growing and permanent in Christ. We thank you for your faithfulness to us, and ask that you would enable us to be faithful to one another. In Christ's name, Amen.

CHAPTER 8

The Pierced Ear Christian

*However, if the servant says to you, "I do not want to leave you," because
he loves you and your household, since he is well off with you, you shall
take an awl and pierce a hole through his ear to the door. Then he will
become your servant permanently…*
DEUTERONOMY 15:16–17

So many people today think that freedom is being able to do
as you please. There isn't any freedom in that. Many of us
have exercised our freedom to do as we please and it hasn't
produced any true freedom at all. Instead it has produced bondage,
scars, hurt, and misery. The only real freedom that anybody can have
is the freedom God offers us in Christ. Jesus Himself said, "If the Son
makes you free, you'll be free indeed" (John 8:36).

If we go to Hebrews 10, we can find out more about what Jesus
means by this. In verses 5-7 the writer is quoting a Psalm, but he puts
the words in the mouth of Jesus. Listen to what He says:

> So when He (Christ) came into the world, he said, "Sacrifice
> and offering you did not desire, but a body you prepared for
> me. Whole burnt offerings and sin-offerings you took no
> delight in." Then I said, "Here I am: I have come—it is written

of me in the scroll of the book—to do your will,
O God."   Hebrews 10:5–7 NET

When Jesus came into the world He said to His father, "sacrifice
and offerings you did not desire." Those are the external, ritualistic
things that men do, often thinking that the ritual itself brings them
closer to God. Jesus tells us that God isn't really concerned about all
of those things. God's original purpose in making humanity was not
so that He could make a bunch of rules, let alone a bunch of rituals,
for mankind to follow. God wouldn't get all His pleasure about a
person keeping the rules and man going through all the motions.
God didn't make a man for that. In sacrifice and in offerings He
takes no pleasure.

We can all practice a ritual without our hearts being in it. We
might just go through the motions: You say a creed. You walk an aisle.
You practice in some sacrament. All of that has its place but those
practices are not central to what God desires from us. He wants us,
like Jesus, to be free to do His will, to do what is pleasing to Him.

Jesus goes on to say, "A body you prepared for me." "I have a
body, I am a human being," Jesus is saying. Jesus is God, but He is
also human. Jesus used His human body to do what was pleasing to
the Father. Jesus was written about in the Scroll of the Book (that is
the Old Testament, the Hebrew Scriptures) and they too revealed
that He had come to do the will of the Father.

Until the Lord Jesus came into this world, there wasn't any man
or woman that was truly free since the fall of Adam and Eve in the
very beginning. When Adam and Eve exercised their option and
rebelled in the Garden, they stepped out of life and into death,
spiritual death. That death passed to all people. When the Lord
Jesus came to this earth, He was conceived miraculously by the
Holy Spirit in the borrowed womb of a virgin Jewish girl. He was
born without that Sin Nature that you and I have from our natural
birth. Jesus was truly free.

The first person to walk this earth truly free since Adam and
Eve fell was the Lord Jesus Christ. What did the first free man since

Adam do with his freedom? He gave it to His father: "I've come to do Your will" Jesus says in there in Hebrews 5:7. "I'm free but I use my freedom to do Your will God," that is what Jesus is saying.

Listen to what Hebrews 9:13-14 tells us about this:

> 13 For if the blood of goats and bulls and the ashes of a young cow sprinkled on those who are defiled consecrated them and provided ritual purity, 14 how much more will the blood of Christ, who through the eternal Spirit offered himself without blemish to God, purify our consciences from dead works to worship the living God.

What I would like for you to pay attention to here is in 9:14: Jesus offered Himself without blemish to God through the eternal Spirit. The eternal Spirit is The Holy Spirit. The Holy Spirit is a co-equal member of the Godhead with the Father and the Son. Through the Holy Spirit, God makes Himself available to men and women. But the Holy Spirit is also the person through whom a person can offer his or her humanity to God. That is what Jesus the man did; He offered himself without spot to God through the Holy Spirit.

If you are a Christian, you have the Holy Spirit. If you don't have the Holy Spirit you do not belong to God, you are not one of His children. The gift of the indwelling presence of the Holy Spirit is the greatest of the birthright blessings that our Heavenly Father has given to us to give us security and empowerment on our life journey. The Holy Spirit living in you enables you to present your humanity to God in order to do His will, the things that are pleasing to Him and the things that will set you free.

Set Free to be Enslaved

I would like to take you to Deuteronomy 15. If you look that up in your Bible, your pages probably won't have any marks or fingerprints; it is a section of the Bible that can often get neglected. In order to understand what is going on here, we need a little background. In this section, God is leading the new generation of Israel into the Promised Land of Canaan. He was repeating to them, "I want you to always remember that you were slaves in Egypt for four hundred years. You were helpless, hopeless, under the tyranny of Pharaoh. You had no military might, no structure, no society—you had nothing and yet, I redeemed you. I brought you out of Egypt by my hand, by my power so that no man can ever take credit for you as a nation. So that you never forget that and always maintain a proper attitude towards Me, I am going to give you some practices so that will always remind you that you are unique, holy among all the other nations."

God gave Israel instructions and laws that related to debts and relationships between fellow Israelites. If you were a Hebrew, an Israelite, and for some reason fell in debt to me and you couldn't pay your debts, God's law made a provision that you could become my slave to work out your debt.

But He also made a provision that every seventh year, debts would be released and slaves would be set free. An Israelite slave would not have to serve more than six years. In the seventh year of your servitude, I would have to release you. All debts were canceled; everybody started with a clean slate.

Think about being enslaved for six years. For six years, 365 days a year you would have to serve your master in whatever he wanted you to do. You would have food and a place to sleep, but you would be enslaved. Now imagine the first day of that seventh year—you are now free. What do you do? How would you use that freedom?

Now your master was supposed to provide for your needs as you started life as a free person again, as the Lord instructed:

> "If you set them free, you must not send them away empty-handed. You must supply them generously from your flock, your threshing floor, and your winepress–as the LORD your God has blessed you, you must give to them. Remember that you were a slave in the land of Egypt and the LORD your God redeemed you; therefore, I am commanding you to do this thing today."   Deuteronomy 15:13–15

All Israel had once been slaves in Egypt but God had set them free and made marvelous provision for them. Just as God had been gracious to Israel, so Israel was to be gracious.

But there was also another option that the Lord provided and that is what I want us to focus on for a minute:

> "However, if the slave says to you, 'I do not want to leave you,' because he loves you and your household, since he is well off with you, you shall take an awl and pierce a hole through his ear to the door. Then he will become your servant permanently (this applies to your female servant as well)."
> Deuteronomy 15:16–17

I want you to imagine with me for a minute how this might have taken place. In the ancient near east, a lot of business was done in the gates of the city. They didn't have courthouses, registrars offices, or title companies the way we do today. If I wanted to make a transaction with someone, to buy some land or a hundred sheep or whatever, we would come and bargain before the elders of the city and the witnesses that were present.

Think about a slave stepping forward and saying, "I fell debtor to my master and I became his slave. I've served him for six years. It's been the best six years of my life. He is the kindest, most benevolent, caring, nurturing master I've ever known. My six years are up and he has set me free. I don't want to be free. I don't want to be free. I want to serve him forever." You can imagine the elders asking him, "Are you under any duress? Is your wife hostage? Are you children being threatened?" It became the slave's burden to convince the elders and the people that this was a voluntary act.

Can you imagine that slave saying, "I know I'm free. The debt's been dealt with, but I love my master. I love his whole house. My whole house loves his whole house. He does a better job of managing me than I ever did managing myself!" Once the slave had proved his point, the elders of the city would take him back against a wooden door and drive an awl right through his ear effectively nailing him to the door. Now that slave's pierced ear would be a sign that he had given himself permanently, a bond-servant of his good, beloved master.

Jesus was born free. What did the Lord Jesus do with His freedom? He backed against the door and said, "Father, Pierce my ear. I always want to do the things that are pleasing to you, I live to do Your will." The only man that was ever truly free used His freedom to become a bond-servant to his father. His "pierced ear" in the process of time led to his pierced hands and his pierced feet and his pierced side. You cannot be forced to be a bond-servant. You have to volunteer. It is amazing to see that Jesus volunteers His freedom in order to become a bond-servant of His Father.

I'm here to tell you that the one primary thing that pleases God in response from your heart to the pierced hands and feet of Christ is your "pierced ear." It's when you voluntarily say to God, "You are such a good Master, I want to serve you forever."

The Price of Redemption

Back in Exodus 15:15 we heard the Lord redeemed Israel out of Egypt. In the New Testament we hear that Christ has redeemed us:

> In Him (Christ) we have *redemption* through His blood, the *forgiveness of our trespasses*, according to the riches of His grace.
>
> Ephesians 1:7

Let me explain to you what redemption means because that is an important idea. In the New Testament one of the backgrounds for the word "redeem" comes from the context of slaves being sold in the market in the Roman empire. Now lets suppose that I owned a slave. I had the title deed to him. He's my slave; I own him. I come to the marketplace and I'm going to put my slave up for sale. The bidding starts and it goes $50, $80, $100. We get the price up to where I want it and I say, "Okay, we have a deal!" The bidding ends. Now I take the title deed and sign the slave over to the new owner.

Now, what happened to my slave in all this? Well, nothing happened to him except that he got traded. He was a slave to me when he entered the market, now he's a slave to the high bidder as he leaves. He didn't get to pick the price, he didn't get to pick who got the high bid. He didn't get to decide who his master was before he was sold or after he was sold. He is a piece of property.

Redeem means not only to pay the price but also to purchase. Now when this word comes over to the New Testament another idea is added in—to pay a price *in order* to set free. That is what the Lord Jesus did when He went to the Cross to redeem you. He paid the price to release you, to free you from slavery to sin, death and the devil (the Bible tells us we were slaves to all three).

Jesus does an amazing thing with your "title deed." You see He paid the price, wrote "paid in full" on your deed and handed it to you. In Galatians, Paul says,

> For freedom *Christ has set us free*. Stand firm, then, and do not be subject again to the yoke of slavery.   Galatians 5:1

The minute you became a Christian you became free indeed. No one can be forced into bondage to Jesus Christ. And God knows that only by setting us truly free will we be able to give ourselves freely and entirely to Him.

So the question becomes, *what will we do with our freedom*? Notice in that Galatians passage that Paul implies that we might even misuse our freedom and fall back into slavery. In Romans Paul tells us the best way we can use our freedom:

> Therefore I appeal to you, brothers and sisters, by the mercies of God, to present your bodies as a sacrifice—alive, holy, and pleasing to God–which is your reasonable service of worship.
> Romans 12:1

In the Letter to the Romans, Paul spends eleven chapters explaining all that God has done for them (and us) and then says, "I appeal to you." He doesn't command, He appeals. Just as in the Deuteronomy passage, you cannot be commanded to become a bond-servant: It's voluntary. The "pierced ear" cannot be commanded. It is an option to every Christian to have your "ear pierced," spiritually speaking—to bind yourself to Jesus as your Master. This is what Paul is appealing for all of us to do.

Notice that Paul is appealing "because of the mercies of God." He wants us to act based on our response to all that Father God has done for us. And then he makes his appeal: "that you present your body a living sacrifice." In other words, give yourself freely as a bond-servant of Jesus Christ. Paul himself had done this. Peter did it. Look at the way they begin some of their letters in the New Testament:

Simeon Peter, a slave and apostle of Jesus Christ...
2 Peter 1:1

Paul, a slave of Christ Jesus, called to be an Apostle..."
Romans 1:1

Some of your translations may have "servant" instead of "slave" but the idea is the same: these men who knew Jesus deeply had freely given their lives in total service to Him. Jesus had set them free and they had become His "slaves."

Where Paul says "present your bodies..." means that he is calling for a decisive action. When a slave said to his master, "I love you and want to serve you forever," that was a one time decision that would have consequences for the rest of his life. Once he had made that commitment, his life would take a certain course. Paul here is calling us to make that type of commitment. He is telling us that the best thing that we can do with our freedom is freely give ourselves to our good Master.

Pierced ear Christians are the only ones that God can get to move when He wants something done. As I serve on committees or just teach the Bible, people will say, "Do I have to do that?" I can honestly say, "No you don't have to do it." I know when people say that, they don't yet have their "ears pierced." The "pierced ear Christians" are those who long ago gave their freedom to Jesus. They are the ones who will say, "If God wants it, He's got it. Tell me what to do. I will do it." They're the Christians who are fun to be around. The "pierced ear Christian" is someone who understands that Christ has set them free and they voluntarily give that freedom to Him, to be His bond-servant.

The world doesn't need to see Christians who just practice Christianity. When they see someone with a pierced ear—like Peter, like Paul, like Jesus—they start to see what it means to be "free indeed." When we give ourselves over to Christ, we discover this as well. True freedom is not being free to serve ourselves, but being free to serve Christ. As we serve Him, we discover that we are truly, eternally free.

I want you to understand clearly that no one can command you to do this. Don't let anyone intimidate you. Don't let anyone badger you. Paul appeals; I appeal to you to. Our Master Jesus, the one we love, exercised His option when He was on earth and gave His freedom over to His Father; He was a "pierced ear" bond-servant of God. Are you greater than your Master? Pierced ear Christians simply say, "*I love my Master. I want to be His bond-servant forever.*"

Prayer

Father, we thank you for the truth that sets us free so that we can serve you. We thank you for the example of our Lord Jesus who lives always to please You. We thank you for the redemption that comes to us in Him. Through the empowerment of your Holy Spirit, help us to fully surrender our lives to You, not out of fear or duress, but out of love. Help us all to see how free we can become we give ourselves to be "enslaved" to Christ. We pray that for all those who are hungry in heart. In Christ's name, Amen.

CHAPTER 9

From Pretense to Prayer

"Whenever you pray, do not be like the hypocrites, because they love to pray while standing in synagogues and on street corners so that people can see them. Truly I say to you, they have their reward.
MATTHEW 6:5

Prayer is one of the most difficult subjects to talk about because people assume you are holding yourself up as having arrived in prayer. I want to clear that up right at the beginning: I am student of prayer and I have learned there's still a lot to learn.

There seems to be a conspiracy of silence about prayer among Christians. If you ask, many will say, "Oh yes—prayer—I understand that." The silence comes in if you go just below the surface and ask, "Are you really satisfied with your prayer life?" The initial reaction is, "Oh sure, yeah. I praise God!" That is what we are supposed to say. But if you push a little deeper and are honest and say, "Well can I say that I am not really satisfied with my prayer life sometimes," you will often get the response, "Well, now that you bring it up, mine is a little bit empty and there are times when I ..."

As Christians, we know we should pray and that we ought to have a good prayer life. We don't want to be perceived as someone who is less than satisfied with that area of our lives. Certainly I don't want to appear less than all that I could be. So we just try to save face.

When I first became a Christian, I was told we needed to pray. Now, I had prayed before that. I used to pray before every football game in high school and college; I would pray that we would win and they would lose! That we wouldn't get hurt and some of them would get creamed! We prayed particularly if it was late in the game and the score was close. I prayed all the time but I didn't understand what true prayer was really about.

After I became a Christian I began to ask, "Why should I pray? What is prayer?" I know that sounds silly to you but I asked those kind of questions. I still do, 28 years later. I ask questions like that and I want to know, *"What's the object of the exercise?"*

Those who were spiritually parenting me at that time said prayer is simply talking to God. That made sense. Prayer is me talking to God. Prayer is any dialog between man and God. It doesn't matter whether your eyes are closed or whether you are riding down the street in your car or whether you are on your knees in your closet or in an open assembly. Any dialog between a man and God is prayer.

That led me to the next question, "What do you think He wants to talk about?" At that point they said, "Well, we have this little formula for you, It's called ACTS: Adoration, Confession, Thanksgiving and Supplication. Just remember that. When you pray just work through those steps." I am sure many of you have heard of this.

I thought, "Well, that's neat and I can certainly learn that." I began to do that for a while but then there came a day I wondered if that could be satisfying to God because it sure wasn't satisfying to me. I began to wonder if I were missing something. So I began to ask, "Lord what is prayer about? Really, what is prayer about?" That's when I began to make some discoveries.

You see, I had let this little routine just become routine. As I adored God, I wondered "Do I really need to keep telling God about Himself?" It is wonderful to praise God, but when it becomes just a routine, it loses something. When I got to confession I was thinking,

What God showed me is what I will share with you here. It is by no means exhaustive, but hopefully it will be helpful to you. I want to share what God taught me as he took me through the school of prayer in my own journey. I want to focus on moving from pretense to meaningful prayer. We are going to talk about what prayer is not and then move on to making meaningful prayer a reality in your life.

Lord Teach Us To Pray

Now Jesus was praying in a certain place, and when He finished, one of His disciples said to Him,
"Lord, teach us to pray, as John taught his disciples."
Luke 11:1

Jesus' first disciples were familiar with prayer; they had prayed from their childhood. But in the course of their time together with Jesus they had taken note of the way He prayed—often alone and not in the way that the Pharisees prayed. So in Luke 11:1 they ask Him how to pray.

Something had got their attention about the way Jesus prayed. I don't think it was His posture or the eloquence of His words—the Gospels record so little about those. I think what the disciples were seeing was the *reality* of His praying. Maybe when Jesus had finished praying one of the disciples realized that His time alone with His Father wasn't an ordeal. Although prayer was an absolutely essential and meaningful part of His life, Jesus didn't treat it like a requirement.

Already Jesus had taught them that prayer was not to be done for public show, but in private:

"And when you pray, you must not be like the hypocrites. For they love to stand and pray in the synagogues and at the street corners, that they may be seen by others. Truly, I say to you, they have received their reward.

But when you pray, go into your room and shut the door and pray to your Father who is in secret. And your Father who sees in secret will reward you."
Matthew 6:5-6

The hypocrites are the pretentious prayers who like to put on a good show for everyone to see. All they wanted to do was to have people hear them and that is all that really happens. Nothing really takes place between them and God the Father.

Jesus gives us all insight into the kind of prayer that God seeks and desires: private, secret prayer. The Father will meet you in secret there in your "prayer closet." As you pray in secret the Father will reward you openly.

That turns us to Luke 11. The disciples couldn't stand it any longer. While they were panicked and always worried about something, Jesus was panic proof. Having been alone with His Father early in the morning, His disciples throughout the course of the day could hear Him saying continually, "Thank you Father. Thank you Father."

Faith is What Prayer is All About

The first "secret" that I have discovered about prayer is that it is about faith. Faith is an attitude. It's a disposition that you have towards God. Faith is an attitude that allows God to do for you what you cannot do for yourself. Faith doesn't get you busy—it gets God busy on your behalf.

When I go to see my dentist and exercise faith in him, that faith doesn't get me busy it gets the dentist busy. I have no idea how to fix my teeth. I go to my dentist because I have faith in him; I trust that he knows what he is doing. So he puts one of those nitrous masks on my nose and pretty soon I am comatose, incapacitated. There is nothing I could do even if I wanted to.

So faith doesn't get you active, it gets someone else active. If you could do what needed to be done, you wouldn't have to have faith in anybody else. But faith comes into play when I get to a point when I can't. That's when we all have to turn to somebody or something to do for us what we cannot do for ourselves.

If I have to go to Vancouver from Memphis, I can't get to British Columbia in a day by any of my own efforts. I have to trust a pilot and an airplane to get me there. I will buy a ticket for a plane that is not even at the airport yet. When I get to the Memphis airport, if I were to ask, "Can I see the plane I am flying on?" More than likely they will say, "It isn't here yet." So I trust that my plane will arrive at the airport at the right time. Pretty soon the plane shows up, I get on the plane and by the afternoon I am in Vancouver. All along the flight, I have to trust that the plane will stay in the air flying like it is suppose to.

Now let me ask you, did I fly to Vancouver by faith? No, I flew by airplane—It's much safer! All my faith did was to get me on the airplane to let the airplane get me to Vancouver. Hopefully you are getting my point by now. Faith is simply your attitude or your disposition that trusts somebody or something to do for you what you cannot do for yourself. That's faith.

When you realized that you could not save yourself, you decided to put your faith in Christ. Did that get you busy? No, it got Christ busy. The minute you said, "I can't but you can and I'll let you," Christ redeemed you. Your faith simply allowed Christ to do for you what you could never do for yourself. Faith and trust are essential to most things we do in life and prayer is no exception.

Nowhere do we find this reality more, than in prayer. Prayer is an exercise of faith. It comes out of a trustful disposition and attitude. It is easy to think yourself right out of faith, especially in prayer. But you need to understand that your Heavenly Father wants to hear from you. You don't need to beg God. You don't need to persuade Him or twist His arm or somehow convince Him. He longs to hear from His children.

Abraham in the School of Prayer

God tells us in the Bible about some people that He calls friends. I want to be a friend of God. I am His child and we all begin there but being His child is the first step in becoming His friend. Becoming His friend takes time just like being anyone's best friend takes time. Anyone who is your best friend has earned that right over many years. God called Abraham His friend and He called Moses His friend. By following the teachings of Jesus, we too become His friends (see John

15:14-15). We are redeemed, but we can also become His friends: people who faithfully do what pleases Him.

Abraham was a friend of God, but Abraham had to learn how to pray. I don't mean that Abraham didn't know how to say prayers; Abraham had to learn the reality of faithful praying. I'd like for you to think about this story.

The problems had gotten really bad in Sodom and Gomorrah. In Genesis 18:17 the Lord said, "Shall I hide from Abraham what I am about to do." In effect, the Lord was saying, "Abraham's my friend. I don't hide things from my friends." God has come down to bring judgment on two very wicked cities, Sodom and Gomorrah.

The first thing I want you to learn about prayer is that in any dialog man to man—let alone man to God—the authority, the expert should do all the talking. Imagine you and I going to NASA and meeting all the chief engineers, seeing all their control rooms, launch pads and rockets. When we finish the tour, the engineers tell us about what they do. Now imagine me just jumping up and saying, "Wait, let me tell you about it!" After I rehearsed all that I knew, one of you might get up and tell all that you knew. Now what would we accomplish that afternoon? We would just expose our ignorance. That's all we'd do. The engineers might indulge us with a polite smile, but when we left, they'd look at one another and say, "They haven't got a clue!"

When you are talking to the God of the universe, prayer involves letting the authority do the talking. When you go into your closet, be quiet. Prayer is first listening to a friend who wants to talk to you about something He knows all about. We always go racing in, panicked, dead set to tell God, "I know you don't know this, but did you know that the President is thinking about ... and my gosh, and if this health plan ... Did you know that?" We just run on and on as if God is saying, "Nooooo, really!?"

What would be more exciting to Him is if you came and said Lord, "Thank you that you are in total control. You're not sitting on the edge of your seat. You don't wait for *USA Today* or *The Wall Street Journal* to find out what is going on in the world. You already know.

I'm your child. I just want to get close to you." We are getting close now to what prayer is about. The authority always does the talking.

You see, Abraham—who is the father of faith, a spiritual giant—didn't know any more than us. So in Genesis 18:1 God appeared to Abraham by the oaks of Mamre. Abraham looked up and there were three men coming to him. He ran out to them and bowed down before them. He bowed down because he recognized these were angelic beings—messengers from God. In reality it was a pre-incarnate appearance of Christ and two angels with Him. Abraham said,

> "O Lord, if I have found favor in your sight, do not pass by your servant. Let a little water be brought, and wash your feet, and rest yourselves under the tree, while I bring a morsel of bread, that you may refresh yourselves, and after that you may pass on—since you have come to your servant."
>
> So they said, "Do as you have said." Genesis 18:3–5

Abraham scurried around because he recognized he was in the divine presence. He scurried around trying to be as hospitable as possible and then they ask him, "Where is Sarah, your wife?" He said, "She's in the tent." Then the Lord said to Abraham, "I will surely return to you this time next year, and your wife Sarah will have a son!" (Genesis 18:10). Sarah was standing behind the flap, inside the tent. She could overhear the conversation. At that point, the story reminds us, "Abraham and Sarah were old and advancing in years; Sarah had long since passed the time for having children." (Genesis 18:11)

Now when Sarah heard what was said, she laughed. She laughed inside, not outside, not even a snicker, not a whimper. She laughed within herself:

> So Sarah laughed to herself, saying, "After I am worn out, and my lord is old, shall I have pleasure?" Genesis 18:12

Abraham was 99 at the time of this story. He and Sarah had long ago given up. In fact, they had tried a few years earlier to get God out of a pickle and Ishmael was born to Abraham through Hagar, but that was not God's plan to fulfill His promise. They tried to help God with His plans and they produced all that a man in his own wisdom and power can do for God: *nothing.*

> The LORD said to Abraham, "Why did Sarah laugh and say, 'Shall I indeed bear a child, now that I am old?' Is anything too hard for the LORD? At the appointed time I will return to you, about this time next year, and Sarah shall have a son."
>
> Genesis 18:13–14

Now, when Sarah heard this, she denied that she had laughed. That's hypocrisy. "I didn't do that," Sarah says. "Yes you did," the Lord says. Sarah wasn't a friend to God yet. She knew God. She trusted God for her salvation. She wasn't a friend of God. They weren't there yet. You see the Lord won't allow her hypocrisy and pretense. Friendship to God without worship of God will always lead to contradiction and deceit.

Abraham was embarrassed. He knew then this was a supernatural appearance because his guests could read the very intents of people's heart. At this point, the visitors leave and move toward Sodom and Abraham followed them (Genesis 18:16).

I want you to pay close attention to Abraham, the father of the faith, as he's just now becoming a friend in his 90's. At this point in the story, Abraham began to get busy. He went with the two angels and the Lord Jesus. If you don't know God, you'll tell Him how to get around in His universe.

The Lord had not come to Abraham to get his advice; He had come to let Abraham know what He was about to do:

> The LORD said, "Shall I hide from Abraham what I am about to do, seeing that Abraham shall surely become a great and mighty nation, and all the nations of the earth shall be blessed in him? For I have chosen him, that he may command his children and his household after him to keep the way of the LORD by doing righteousness and justice, so that the LORD may bring to Abraham what he has promised him."
>
> Then the LORD said, "Because the outcry against

Sodom and Gomorrah is great and their sin is very grave,
I will go down to see whether they have done altogether
according to the outcry that has come to me. And if not, I will
know."   Genesis 18:16–20

Now the two "men" left there and went towards Sodom. But Abraham, he stood there with the Lord. Suddenly, Abraham realized that his nephew Lot was in Sodom. And so Abraham began to intercede: "Will you sweep away the godly along with the wicked? (Genesis 18:23)

As Abraham begins to question the Lord, he never mentions Lot. He just asks a question, "Will you destroy the righteous with the wicked?" You know the story. Abraham begins to "bargain" with the Lord: "If there are fifty righteous people in that city will you destroy it? …" Finally, the Lord says that even if there were only ten righteous people in the city, it would not be destroyed. In the end Sodom is so completely wicked it is destroyed and the Lord moves on. Abraham also returns to his home.

Now Abraham has just had a marvelous prayer meeting with the Lord Himself. How much did Abraham accomplish? Absolutely nothing. What did Abraham contribute to that prayer meeting? His ignorance, his immaturity. Abraham had not figured out why God came by his tent in the first place. God didn't come by to debate with Abraham, He came by to tell him what he was going to do because Abraham needed to understand the righteous ways of the Lord so that he would be able to teach his family.

Abraham did all the talking. He didn't do any listening. You won't find Abraham doing that again. The next time God comes by and speaks to Abraham, He's going to say, "You take your son and go up mount Moriah." Abraham says, "Yes sir." As he's going up the mountain, his son keeps asking him, "Father, where's the sacrifice?" Abraham says, "God will take care of that" (see Genesis 22).

In his life-journey Abraham had learned that God does the talking and *Abraham does the listening*. Abraham became a friend of God because he learned to listen. When the writer of Hebrews remembers Abraham, one of the things he says is,

> For when God made a promise to Abraham, since he had no one greater by whom to swear, he swore by himself, saying, "Surely I will bless you and multiply you."
> And thus Abraham, *having patiently waited*, obtained the promise.   Hebrews 6:13–15

The Spirit Intercedes

> In the same way, the Spirit helps us in our weakness, for we do not know how we should pray, but the Spirit himself intercedes for us with inexpressible groanings. And He who searches our hearts knows the mind of the Spirit, because the Spirit intercedes on behalf of the saints according to God's will.
>   Romans 8:26–27

In this passage Paul tells us that we really don't know how we should pray. We don't know what we are supposed to pray for. But the Holy Spirit who knows the heart of God intercedes for us. When I learned this truth, I thought, "Haven't I been silly. I'll just give my prayer list to the Holy Spirit. He indwells me. He understands me. He knows my chemistry. He knows me better than I will ever know myself. I will trust His intercession for me!"

From that day until this day when anybody comes up and says to me, "Tom we have a problem. Will you pray with me?" I will look them in the eye and say, "If in my prayer time, the Holy Spirit brings that to my remembrance, I'd be delighted to pray for you."

There are over six billion people in this world and I can't pray for every one of them. There are thousands and thousands of missionaries in the field and I can't pray for all of them. We have all faced the pressures that can be put on us by prayer. People would come to me and say, "What about Nigeria Tom?"

"I hadn't even thought about Nigeria! Yes, they are dying in Nigeria. I'd add Nigeria to my list."

Then someone would come in and say, "What about all the orphans in Memphis?"

I'd say, "Yes. I hadn't even thought about the orphans in Memphis. I need to add those to my prayer list."

Pretty soon I had zillions of things going. I had to write it all down to keep track of it all.

I discovered that if God doesn't bring something to mind, it's not for me to pray about. All of these things I have mentioned and that you can probably think of are good things to be praying about and need to be prayed for. But I can't pray for them all. Neither can you.

What I have learned to do is just get alone with the Lord and be quiet. I say, "Lord, the only thing I want to pray for is what you want me to pray for." I will tell you what happens. When the Lord brings a prayer concern to my heart, there are two things that happen. First, I will let that person know that I prayed for them. I will let them know, by letter or by call. I will say, "This morning, the Lord brought you to my mind and I prayed for you." That keeps me from being hypocritical. Secondly, I know that when the Lord brings something to mind in prayer, He has something for me to do about it. So my next question to Him is, "What do you want me to do? Do you want me to make a call, write a letter, go by and see them, say a word? What do you want me to do?"

When people come and say what about Nigeria? I'll say, "If the Lord brings it to my mind, I will pray for Nigeria." If He doesn't, I'm free because He's got somebody else praying about Nigeria. I'm not big enough to be God, I can't pray for everybody. I can't pray for everything. I just tell people, "I'm glad you shared that with me and if the Lord brings it to my heart, I promise you I will pray and do what He leads me to do."

I can't tell you the relief that I've gotten from learning that the Holy Spirit, has our real prayer list and He will bring to mind the things that we should be praying about. The things that He brings to our mind to pray about are the things He probably wants you to be involved in and so you're going to need some instruction. You then have to say, "Lord, since you're bringing that person to my mind, I also need to know what you want me to do?" Then you do it. You don't have to get your pastor's consent; you don't have to check it out with your Sunday School teacher. All you need to do is quietly go and do what the Lord laid on your heart.

I remember one time we had a deacons meeting and we had been cutting our budget at church. One of the things that was cut was the pastor's book allowance which was about $400 a year. That allowance had been given to him so all of his salary could go to support his family.

One of the fellow deacons became very burdened about that and so we called a deacons meeting to see if we could do something. There were some who wanted to put it back in the budget and that would mean that we would have to amend the budget, give 90 days notice to the assembly, convene two hearings ... You know how things often work in churches and committees.

I stood up and said, "Time out! Let's not do that. This gives us a great opportunity to practice what I've been teaching about prayer. God knows exactly what He wants to do, so lets give Him a chance. Let's do what they did in the New Testament. Let's just pray, give thanks, and ask Him what He wants each of us to do."

We just had a short prayer right after the meeting and I said, "Brothers, let's just go home today and pray all afternoon. Just ask God if this is something you are to be concerned with and if it is, what are you to do about it?" I told them to just tell the treasurer what God has told you to do, give what the Lord instructs, and don't discuss it with anybody else. I wanted to see if God were really alive and present with us. I wanted to see what might happen if we take Jesus' teaching at His word: go pray in secret and the Father will reward in the open (Matthew 6:6).

Pretty soon everybody was wondering, "Well, what happened?" I really didn't have a clue. I would say, "Well, did you do what God told you to do?"

"Well, yeah."

"Then, everything happened exactly like it's supposed to."

"Yeah, but what happened did we get any money?"

I said, "Well, God's will was done if you did what God told you to do."

I drove them all nuts. I had instructed the treasurer not to tell anybody, even me, what had happened. He was to take the money and give it to the pastor. That went on for about six weeks and all the deacons almost drove me nuts: "How much did we get?" I was simply trusting that if everybody did what God told them to do, we got all we were supposed to.

Eventually it just got ridiculous. People were putting pressure on the treasurer to find out and anybody who they thought might know. Finally, one of the older deacons couldn't stand it any longer. He said, "Brother Tom, we just have to know!" At that point I relented. I told them we would find out, but that it was not a move of faith. It grieves me that we can't just rest in God. It grieves me that we always have to know what's happening.

We called a deacon's meeting and it was packed. I asked, "Did everybody in this room do what God told them to do? If you didn't, you need to come see the treasurer and give him some money real quick." Everybody sat still.

I said, "Well, what did we give? The treasurer said just a little over $2800.

The old deacon said, "What did we do with the surplus?"

I said, "Brother, there wasn't any."

"You gave that preacher $2800!?" he responded.

I said, "Brother, did you do what God told you to do?"

He said, "Well I think I did."

I said, "Well then the preacher got exactly what he was supposed to have. Did it ever dawn on you that $400 a year might have been too low to begin with?"

He said, "That preacher shouldn't get that much money!!!"

Well I am convinced that God thought our preacher should get that money and so He led us to give. That was interesting episode; I had a lot of fun with that one!

When I teach on prayer, I say, "Don't seek His hand, seek His face." The real secret in prayer is learning to listen. Once we know what the Lord wants, we can follow Him as He leads.

Prayer

Father we thank you that you want to hear from us as your children in prayer. We thank you for the truth that sets us free from pretentious, hypocritical prayer lives. We often get so busy throwing words at you, that we forget we should be listening. Father help us to remember that You're the authority. We need your Spirit who is helping us in our weakness. Father tell us what you want to do and what role you want us to play. We want to rejoice in just spending time with you, seeking your Face until we trade faith for sight. Until then, may our lives be truly pleasing to you. In Christ's name, Amen.

CHAPTER 10

From Routine to Reality

> *"Look carefully then how you walk,*
> *not as unwise but as wise,*
> *redeeming the time,*
> *because the days are evil."*
> EPHESIANS 5:15–16

Let me talk to you about the way the Lord has operated in my life. I am one of those individuals that has to know "why" about everything. It got me in a lot of trouble as a kid. I wanted to know how a clock worked or how a radio worked and I took them apart. We had bags of radios and clocks that were never put back together. I could never figure out how to get them back together.

When I became a Christian at 26, I caused a lot of problems to some very sincere Christians because I wanted to know the "why" of everything. I happened to have been converted at a Baptist Church. I was 26, biblically illiterate and every time I asked a question, I was told what Baptists believed. I didn't really care what Baptists or anybody else believed; I really just wanted to know the truth and so I would continue to ask all these questions. People were a little bit irritated and so they gave me a book called *What Baptists Believe* and thought that would get rid of me. That didn't get rid of me. I still had a lot of questions and I wanted answers I could understand.

After a few frustrating years, God began to put the question in my heart, "Why don't YOU start looking for the answers?" I don't consider myself exceptional by any means. I think there are many people that are much brighter than I am, with better analytical skills. I long to see those people get exposed to the truth of Scripture, to see their eyes light up and for them to go into orbit. I'm always aware that many of the people who are sitting in my classes will probably do in one year what it took me five years to do once they grasp the truth and begin to grow. I never get the idea that I am the authority or by any means the example. I know sitting in front of me, particularly in college groups, there are kids that are so bright. Once they grasp the truth in Christ, they will take off and hit new heights.

I have a son who is 21 who spent the first six weeks of this summer in Russia with Campus Crusade and he's now out on the book field with Thomas Nelson, getting some experience. I had to write him today. I told him you're just blowing me away. He's already led several of his fraternity brothers to Christ. He's been on a mission trip to Russia. He's studying his Bible and has a devotional time every day. It just blows me away to think where he is at 21 and that he will roar past me. I'm glad. I'm happy. I couldn't be more content. No telling where he'll be by the time he is my age. I am in awe of all those who come to know Christ early and really get fired up.

Five Things You Can Do

As I have said, I was very zealous about making my life count for Christ after my initial salvation. Early on I was told to just get active in church. Now there are five things you can do in most any church and go right to the top. You can do all five of them without Christ.

The first thing you have to do is just be there every time the doors are open. Your attendance record is seen as a measure of your commitment to Christ. I did that. If the first grade choir sang, I was there with all the grandparents even though I didn't have children in the choir, I was there because we were required to be there. But that was a sign of my commitment.

The second thing you have to do is get into the Word. That usually means get you a King James or an NIV, red lettered edition of course, and one of those zipper cases and carry it around with you everywhere. Now you don't ever have to read it, just have it so that everybody knows you have all the right stuff. You don't ever read for yourself, just have it there on Sunday morning when someone says, "Turn in your Bible to …" If you are really serious, you can get involved in a Bible class. Now you're "in the Word." You may be as biblically illiterate as I was, but you're in the Word.

The third thing you have to do is give some money on a consistent basis. Just consistently give. Now only God, your accountant and you know if you are actually practicing stewardship, but that doesn't matter. Everyone else *sees* that you are giving.

Now you have to get involved. That is the fourth thing you need to do. You can park cars on Wednesday night or you can pass out Kool-Aid at Vacation Bible School or you can hand out brochures in your ladies study group but you must get involved.

The fifth and final thing to do is just be patient. That probably is the hardest thing, but if you are patient, you will soon get promoted up the ladder. In our church we had nominating committees. The nominating committees meet to see who can fill all the responsibilities. I later got to be on a nominating committee and I found out how it works. The church would have a need and someone, who was doing the five key things, would get nominated: "Hey what about Tom Murray?" Somebody said, "Yeah he's here all the time."

"Is he in the Word?"

"He has an NIV with a zipper case, monogrammed on the outside with the dove wings on it—You know he is in the Word."

"Does he tithe?"

"We checked—every week. There's an envelope every week."

"Is he involved, is he serving?"

"Well, yeah, we know he's at the back. He ushers every Sunday."

"Well what are we waiting for? He meets all the criteria. Anybody know where he is?"

That's how you get nominated. That's what happened to me—I became the biblically illiterate chairman of the deacon body of a large church. Every fourth Sunday of the month we met and we would go over the financial accounts. They'd say, "You know account 507b, postage is over $10.00." We could get 30 minutes of discussion out of that. Someone else would say, "Did you know the paint was peeling on the back steps?" I dreaded every fourth Sunday, every month because we had to get three hours of deacon's meetings in and all we could do is crunch numbers and talk about things that nobody cared about. When we left, everybody dropped their agenda in the garbage can and it was never heard of again. I had gone right to the top, but I was miserable.

As I would look around the room, I began to realize everybody was as miserable as I was. Some of them had been doing that for 40 years. I began to think, "God, if that's all there is to the Christian life, I quit." Now I knew I was going to Heaven, but in the meantime, I was having a mean time. I somehow knew there had to be more.

Now in time, sincere people—including me—would have a crisis or a moment in their life when they realized that they were dry and something needed to happen. We would have altar calls or times when you could make personal commitments and we would go to the front of the church. You would tell the Lord that you weren't pleased with the quality of your walk with him. You really meant business and that you really wanted to see a change in your life. There would be tears, genuine tears. I shed some of those. Then you would go back to your pew and within months there would be literally absolutely no evidence that you had been to the front or that anything had really changed.

I thought that was interesting because I believed those people are sincere. I believed their tears were genuine—mine were. Yet, three months, six months later, no change. Finally, I thought, "I'm not going down there anymore. They can give all the altar calls they want, it isn't going to work. Why should I go? Just to go down to get my hopes up again, rededicate my life, only to go back 90 to 120 days later and still have the frustration of no change." I knew that was not right.

But that put my wheels to turning. "Why? Why are we doing this? What's wrong when that happens?" Maybe you've done that. I have found over the years that there are people sitting in our churches who hear all kinds of opportunities to express themselves to Christ, to come forward to commit their life, to walk in front and they don't move. Many times, I know why. They've already been down there, again and again. They've done it beside their bed. They've done it in their office. They've said it in their cars. They've been to the pastor's study. They've visited counselors but nothing happened. So they just quit. Many of our pews are filled with Christians who are just killing time until time kills them. They're just existing. God never intended for us to live that way.

The Rut Routine

As I was trying to figure out what was going on with all this I learned something: we are all creatures of habit. We see it in the way we do everything. Some of us dress by putting our pants on first, then socks. Some put socks on first, then pants. Some shave then shower, others shower then shave—we all have our little routines to everything we do throughout the day. Most of the time you are not even really aware of what you are doing or how you are doing it, until someone messes up your rhythm, your sequence.

The problems is that as creatures of habit we can get into bad habits just like we can get into good habits. We all have our routines and a routine is wonderful until it becomes a rut. Do you know what a rut is? A rut is a grave with both ends kicked out. So a routine can be your servant but a rut can be your death.

We can all get in ruts, particularly with God and our spiritual walk. When we get in a rut, it doesn't take long before we know we need to get out. So we come forward, we rededicate our lives, we pray a prayer—but many times we are not sincere. To get out of the rut, we have to change our routine.

I would like for you to think about something with me for a minute. We all follow a basic routine and that is the cycle of our week. Imagine running around a track. The track represents your week—you start "running" on Monday and come to an end on Sunday night. I think that is pretty normal for most of us. That week is one full loop around the track.

Now if you think about literally running around a track, you know it is going to take time and energy. So lets imagine we all start running around a track. Some of us might get ahead of some of the others depending on what kind of shape we are in. After a while, some of you might start to get fatigued and say, "I am running out of energy, I am slowing down, I want to stop." Now I look back and say, "Listen, you are just not trying hard enough. You need to commit, pick up the pace." You take my advice and instead of stopping, you just run a little bit harder. All that means is you are going to get where I am a little bit faster and a lot more tired.

After a little bit you are barely able to speak but you say, "I'm dying! I don't think I can do this anymore!" Again I say, "Your problem is that you're not committed. You need to try harder." If you continue to follow my advice you will literally die on that track. If you spend physical energy, fatigue will come in until finally it will destroy your body.

The same is true of our spiritual lives. When people come to the front and say, "I'm fatigued with life. I'm tired. I'm wiped out. I'm fried. My hair is on fire. I'm frustrated," and we say, "You just need to try harder. You need to get more involved in church," we are really just giving them a death sentence. You're going to kill them doing that. You'll put them back in the game when they're exhausted. They're telling you they're exhausted and you put them back in the game. Six months later you won't even find them; they'll leave church. They'll stay home. They can't take it.

We all know that if we spend physical energy we get physically fatigued. When we spend emotional, mental and spiritual energy, we also get spiritually fatigued. You can do that just sitting in a pew, worrying, fretting, struggling. There is another word for this spiritual fatigue and we call it depression.

When people come for counseling and say, "I'm at wits end!" the worst thing that they can be told is, "You need to get busy." When we reach that point of spiritual exhaustion, we need help. I know many Christians who are this point: they are emotionally depressed and yet they are being told to try harder. They just don't have anything to give and they are made to feel guilty.

We all live in this cycle of a week. Let me tell you what happens. People who live in this rut, suddenly come out of this cycle because they realize there is a real need in their life. They come to Christ to recommit, to rededicate, to do something with their life to make it count. Then, the reason that nothing happens is they come from that valid commitment, right back to the same cycle. Nothing changes. If nothing changes in this cycle, nothing will happen as a result of that commitment.

Commitment Leading to Change

So the question becomes, what can we do to make real change? The first thing that I want you to really understand is that any commitment you make in your life to God should change the pattern of your week. If you make a commitment to God and go back to the same rut—the same routine you have been living in up to that point—nothing will change. Time will not make a difference. Nothing will happen 30, 60, 90, 100 days later if you don't change the way you are moving through your week.

So let's think about our track again—the cycle of our week. I found that when I'd come to the end of my week—Friday for my business, Sunday for church and spiritual things—I always felt frustrated and guilty. If I had a good week in business, I hadn't spent enough time with my family and they let me know it. Somehow if I could have a real good week in my business and spend some quality time with my family, I hadn't spent any time with God. If I could figure out how to have a good week in business, spend time with my family and spend some time with God, I hadn't had any time for myself. I don't get to fish or play golf, take a walk. I was frustrated about that. If I could figure out how to have a good week in business, spend some quality time with my family, spend some time with God, and have some personal time, the church said you're not helping us enough. If I could figure out how to have a good week in business, spend some quality time with my family, spend time with God and have time for myself, and get down to the church, I realized I had not talked to my mom and my brother and my sister. If I happened to have done all that, then Jeannie my wife would say, "When are we ever going to have any time alone?" Can you relate to this? I was very frustrated. I just wanted to quit. But that frustration became a classroom for me.

At that point, I thought about two possibilities that addresses this problem. The first possibility is that God is unreasonable. I thought, "He's given me more to do than the time to do it. I don't have enough time." Have you ever said or thought that? Basically it is saying that God is unreasonable. He's asked you to be in business, to be a married partner, to be a parent, to stay in touch with your church and your church family, to have your own time—and you really don't have time to do all that!

The second possibility that I considered is that I'm not using my time wisely. None of us like to admit that. I hated it. But that is the option that I realized made the most sense. So the question now becomes, "How can I use my time more wisely?"

Redeem the Time

"Look carefully then how you walk, not as unwise but as wise, redeeming the time, because the days are evil. Therefore do not be foolish, but understand what the will of the Lord is."
Ephesians 5:15–17

Read those verses above carefully. We are going to use those as the basis to talk about some practical things we can do to use our time more wisely. First of all, notice that this all revolves around redeeming the time because the days are evil. Now what does Paul mean, "because the days are evil?" In my own experience I have discovered that Satan will entice you to misuse your time so that you will neglect God's will for your life. Satan will get you so busy doing good things in your church, in your business, in your own life that your whole life will get out of balance.

Notice also that we do all of this, not in foolishness, but understanding what the will of the Lord is. What does that mean? Practically, this means getting our priorities lined up the way God wants us to in a way that is best for us. I am going to suggest that He wants you to get a good night's rest, have quality time with God and with your family, have plenty of time for your business, have time for fellowship with believers, and have time to relax. He has given you all the time you need to do this if you can simply say, "Father, show me what needs to go and what needs to be added so that my schedule lines up with *Your* schedule." You will be in balance and you will know the will of God. Let's talk about how we do that practically.

We all live in a cycle of a week. You can think about that in terms of our running track illustration. So on Monday, you begin the "race": soccer, ladies club, nails done at 11:30—the list goes on. By Monday night you are exhausted. Then comes Tuesday and Tuesdays are a terror. You move on through the days and finally get to the "finish line"—Sunday—and that is the worst day. You may be running from sunup to sundown. I almost looked forward to Mondays. Sunday was intense with church and meetings and all kinds of things.

All of us have only 24 hours a day, seven days a week which is 168 hours. That's all we have. If you would think of that as your salary in time, that's all you get paid. We all get "paid" that same amount. If the president of General Motors is getting more done in a week than you and I are isn't because he has more time; it's because he manages his time better.

Nobody was ever more pressed that Jesus Christ. Did you ever realize in the 30+ years he was on this earth, he never had more than 168 hours in a week? He was never late, never in a panic and He accomplished everything He was supposed to do in His Father's will. That eliminates the idea that God is unreasonable in the amount of time He has given us. So it comes back down to you and me—how will we use the time that God has given us. Paul says we need to learn how to redeem the time. I learned to be teachable about how I use this 168 hours in the cycle of my week. We all need to learn how to manage this time.

I want to share something with you that I call a time budget. The first thing to learn is a time budget is your servant and not your master. It doesn't tell you what to do, it just helps you know when you are going to do what you do. It's the same with a financial budget. If you have $50 discretionary per week, the budget doesn't tell you can't have pizza. It just lets you know that if you spend $15 on pizza, you have $35 left. When your budget tells you are out of money, you can get mad at it, but it is just telling you the truth.

As we think about this 168 hours in our time budget, the first thing we have to do is establish our priorities. Priority One would be whatever you would do if you were absolutely sure that by this time next week you would be dead. What would you do? Would you try to increase your third, fourth quarter earnings in your corporation? Would you be interested that you got elected to the elders board? Would you really be interested in about 90% of the things that are taking up your time? Probably not. I would dare say that for most people Priority One would be to be sure they are right with God. If God ought to be priority number one in that situation, and He should, then that should be priority one in every moment of your life.

I would suggest that Priority Two needs to be your family. In fact, if you knew you'd be dead in a week you'd have a little prayer with God and then you would gather your family—there would be lots of things to say, lots of things to get straightened out. You should be getting the idea about how I am developing this idea of "redeeming the time"—live today as though it is the last day of your life. We are not trying to be morbid here, but the reality is that none of us know how much time we have so we should redeem each day.

There are two last priorities that I want to suggest to you: your job and your church. Now we can keep on adding to the list from there, but I'm gonna stop there. If you show me someone who has a personal relationship with God, and they are practicing that relationship in family relationships, and they practice their relationship with their family on their job, then local churches would not be able to deal with all the people who would come and want to find out how that was all being done. I believe the world would come to us and want to know how we are making all of that work. The problem is we have many who are putting their job ahead of God, and their Church ahead of their family—including pastors and staff. I know kids who have grown up with parents in the ministry who say, "I don't want anything to do with ministry or the church because these took my dad away from me!"

Even pastors can get in trouble because they put the church and their job ahead of their family. Their wives are in trouble. Their families are in trouble. You owe it to your pastor to make sure that he has these priorities sorted out right and support him as a church. If his priorities are not ordered right, you won't have the pastor you want anyway. If he and his walk with God and his family are not right, you Pastor is cheated and you are cheated.

Now since it's true that we all have 168 hours in the week, the first thing to do practically is sit down and make you a one week calendar. I just drew one on a piece of notebook paper. I drew a simple chart with columns for seven days and charted out how I'm spending my time right now. Monday, I'm usually up at 4:30 AM (don't panic—I'm usually asleep by 9:30), have my quiet time until about 6:30. Nobody interrupts me at 4:30 in the morning. I'm not bothering my family and I've been doing this for 20 something years. That's my personal quiet time. When the kids were in school I would leave about 7:30 for work and I didn't get home until 5:30 so I just called 7:30 to 5:30 work. Then, I'd get home at 6:00 PM and we'd have dinner until about 6:30. Then from about 7 to 9:30 we were doing family things. 9:30 was bed time again. You see the first thing I did was just map out what I was actually doing first.

Setting Priorities

Now what I found out is I was trying to do about 280 hours of work in 168 hours. That's why I was so miserable and so frustrated. I discovered that the problem wasn't that I needed more time, It was that I needed to bring my time into balance with God's plan—His will for me. You remember, "If any man lacks wisdom, let him ask of God who gives to all liberally." He doesn't shame us. He delights in giving us what we need. As I asked for wisdom here is what I learned.

As you are working out your time budget, the first thing you have to do is look at your time and allocate your best time—your most productive time—to Priority Number One. The time when you are at your best should be given to Priority One, in this case your time with the Lord.

Now let me tell you rule number one to get your clock to match God's clock. You never, never, never sacrifice sleep. I know you like that. When you're physically tired you are not mentally alert. You're not emotionally equipped. You are not spiritually rested. If you are physically tired you are running on low fuel and everybody is getting the leftovers.

The first thing God wants a lot of us to do is just go home and go to sleep. Don't feel guilty. When you get really rested you will be able to make time for all these other things. Everyone has an inner clock and only you and God know how long it takes for you to get the sleep and rest you need. You just need to find out what that is. If you're an eight hour sleeper, get your eight. If you're a nine, get your nine. If you are a six, get your six. You need to find out how much sleep you are going to need so that you can be at your best for everything else.

I'm a six hour sleeper—that's all I need. If you try to keep me in bed after six hours, I am like a caged tiger. Now my wife needs a solid nine hours; if you get her up before nine hours, you'll wish you hadn't. I function better when I go to bed early and rise early. My wife functions better going to bed later and rising a little later. That's just the way our clocks work differently. We spent some pretty miserable years with me trying to get her up to see the sunrise and with her trying to get me to see Johnny Carson's opening monologue. We were miserable. When I realized this, I said "Jeannie, don't you understand? We're on different clocks. God didn't make us the same way!" We came to an agreement that worked for us. My wife used to vacuum floors when I was asleep. That's when she would have her quiet time and give God her best time.

At 4:30 in the morning, I am wide awake. I am alert. That's my time with God. I'll get up in the morning and do my studying with God. Then I would fix breakfast for the kids. You guys are going to get mad at me for sharing this, but all the time my kids were in elementary school, I made the breakfast and lunches for my three children. But that was my quality time with my children—that is when I was at my best for Priority Two—family. I was the breakfast bar—the made to order chef. The morning was not my wife's best time. As we were getting ready for school she was comatose. So after I had the kids on the way to school, I would take her coffee and wake her up.

Now come 9:00 PM , when I was unfolding my tent for the night, Jeannie had been picking up the kids from all around, talking with them, watching Johnny Carson and getting into bed around 11:00 or 11:30, long after I was comatose. Once we figured all this out it was great! It's been great ever since. She doesn't see sunrises, and I don't see the Late Show but we see each other when we're at our best.

It takes 21 days to make a habit. I want to challenge you to make an appointment with God and meet with Him at your best time for the next 21 days. You know when your best time is, I don't, so just set that time apart for Him and meet with Him in that best time. I challenge you to try this for 21 days and see what happens. Make your appointment and keep it. This time doesn't have to been long or complicated, but set apart your time and meet with Him.

Our second best time goes to Priority Two which is family. You will have to plan for time with family. I started when mine were in elementary school. I set aside a Friday afternoon for each of my three kids and after school I would pick them up and spend the rest of the afternoon with them doing whatever they wanted.

I started with my oldest daughter, Kristen. At 2:15 she would get in my car all giggly, silly and goose bumpy because dad was taking the time. I had my tie and coat off ready to go. I asked her, " What are we going to do?"

"Whatever you want to do," she said.

"No, no, no. You're in charge. I'm in your world. I want to spend time with you doing what you like to do. We'll go where you want to go and we'll do what you want to do as long as you want to do it. We'll eat where you want to eat. I just want to be in your world."

"Really!"

"Yeah—whatever you want to do."

You know what we did? We bought panty hose. She was just beginning to wear panty hose and so she took me to a lingerie department in a mall. There was a high school girl waiting on us, looking at me, both of us red as beet. My daughter was a master in panty hose I learned a lot about panty hose—whether to get with seams or without—a lot about panty hose. God has a weird sense of humor. That became a Friday ordeal.

Of course every time I came to my son Hunter, he'd say, "Dad can we fish on Friday?" After school I would be there with all the gear, changed into some ragged clothes ready to fish.

We went where they wanted to go and do what they wanted to do.

I challenge you as a parent or grandparent to make an appointment with each of your children and go do what they want to do. You don't set the agenda; just say I'd like to go where you want to go and do what you want to do. They will pick the one thing you hate, I can promise you that! God has a tremendous sense of humor. Do what they want to do and say, "I'm just so excited to be in your world. Show me your world." Instead of trying to always make them fit into yours, get into their world.

It wasn't very long before my wife said, "I don't get any Fridays." So every fourth Friday became mom's Friday—Dad took mom and we did what mom wanted to do: shop or look at houses. I just knew what was coming—the things I hate to do. I finally learned how you deal with that, guys: You stay honest. After 25 years I tell my wife, "I hate to shop and I hate to look at houses but I love to please you."

On her Friday I would tell her I would be there but there were two rules: She had to realize that I hated doing those things and there had to be a time limit. So I didn't pout and shuffle my feet and mumble and look at my clock every 15 minutes the whole time. I got with the program. My wife will bear testimony, when I go shopping I am one of the best. But when I go, I know there is an end to *this purgatory*. I even learned a little bit about shopping and looking at houses. I don't like to do these things, but I love to please my wife.

When she grabs my arm and says, "I know you don't want to be here but I love you for doing that." We want to please the ones we love and love means that we are not selfish but give, even doing the things we don't want to do. That is how we "maintain the wells" like we were talking about earlier.

Priority Three—we have to get our work done, no question about that. I found out if I get up early, that's my best time. I have time with my kids, have breakfast, and get them off to school. Then, I got to work. Then I had time with my wife.

Now once those first three are in line, church gets fit in as well. There were a lot of committees I had to get off. Everybody said, "Well what are we going to do?"

"I don't know but God hasn't given me the time to be on your committees right now," I would say. No committees crumbled. Nothing collapsed. Offering didn't go down. Church attendance didn't fail. Isn't that amazing? Everything wasn't riding on me!

Now this all changes as the children get older, get their own cars—you have to make appointments with them. Now that mine are up and grown and one's off to college, Jeannie and I have an incredible amount of freedom that we didn't have before. Some of you don't have that freedom now, but the cycle does change.

To sum up, we want to set our priorities and allocate the time we need to do them at our best. We make sure we get our rest so that we can spend our best time with God. Now we can take the time to share our love of God with our families. We may ask, "God make me the parent to my family that you want me to be. Teach me to do that." Once those are in place we can go to work, tight with God and family, and your job will make sense. With those in place we will want to fellowship with other believers. You show me men and women who have those priorities set and I'll also show you a lot of people who would like to pattern their life after them.

The Testing of Our Faith

The last thing I want to tell you is that when you get this all down, God will test you. Do you remember Peter talking about the testing of our faith that is more precious than gold purified by fire? (see 1 Peter 1:7) You need to know that you will be tested. .

When I was in business, there was this time when we had been trying to get a loan for one of our motels for over a year. A week came when it was Hunter's Friday and as usual he wanted to go fishing. That was already booked—kids Fridays at 2:15. About 11:00 AM that Friday, one of the partners called me up and said, "You're not going to believe it? The bank just called and they can see us at 1:30; they think we can make this deal."

I told this partner, "I've got a problem, I got a conflict."

"Well then, cancel it!" he says—that is what anyone would normally do.

I said, "You don't understand, I can't do that."

Now, I couldn't tell my partner what my conflict was, that I had a six year old son, first grade, who was waiting for his dad to take him fishing.

He said, "Is there a death in the family?"

"Well, no."

"Then rearrange—Anything short of a death, just rearrange it."

Here is a principle that I learned that is important: you never trade a lower priority for a higher priority. Trust me, God will test you on this one.

Listen I said to my partner, "I'll meet with ya'll tonight after dark. I can meet all day Saturday or all day Sunday. I'll meet midnight or 3:00 in the morning. I just cannot meet this afternoon."

He said, "You're killing this deal!" Remember, this a deal we had been trying to get for over a year.

At this point, I just called the president of the bank. I said, "Listen, I have a problem. I'm sorry but I cannot get out of it. I have another commitment."

He said, "We'll work it out. Don't worry about it."

Now we made the loan and we did get the deal. But that Friday afternoon at a pond out in Shelby County, I want you to know that I looked into the eyes a six year old little boy, dancing around at my legs and I knew, for once in my life, that I was in the right place. Which is more important: to make another deal or to put love in a little boy's heart? I said, "God, I know I am where I ought to be—this is your will for me."

If I had changed my appointment with my son—and that's our tendency—what would I have been communicating to him? I would have been saying, "You are a priority until I have a conflict." That's how you tell your wife and your children where they stand with you. By the way, that's how you tell God where he stands with you. It's the same as you trying to fit Him in just about the time you are about to fall asleep: "Now I lay me, down to sleep …" and you don't know how it ended!

You define reality in terms of action and not words. What we actually do communicates to God and family what our actual priorities are. The way you really communicate with your child or your spouse is by making time to be with them. When you say, "When could I spend some time with you?" you say volumes. You are showing that you care enough to invest some time and not just fill out a stupid old chart; you make time because you really want to. There will be plenty of time to fish, golf, read a book—do whatever it is you do to relax—if you get these first priorities right. You'll discover that.

If we had ministers doing that, I think more of their kids would go into the ministry. Many of those kids run from ministries. I have heard some of these kids, especially from missionary families, say, "I don't want anything that reminds me of what you did, because it robbed me of my dad and my mom. I hate church. I hate everything it did to my family." Some of the most bitter counseling that I have ever done are spouses of ministry staff and their children. They're bitter and I understand why. Nobody did that maliciously or intentionally. It's just that if you don't understand, you get in trouble.

Expect God to test you and the first test that I have when somebody calls me, my challenge in life is to line my seven days up with God's seven days and each of those 24 hours with his 24 hours. Don't think you have tomorrow or the next day. Live as though today were last day of your life, not morbidly but redeem the time today.

When you suddenly sense that you are getting all cluttered up again, getting frustrated, the first thing you should do is call a time out: "God I am getting back in a rut again." You'll probably find that you are skipping your sleep and running on fumes. So get your little chart out and work through the process again. You will have to be willing to cut things out, to call people and say, "I am sorry I just can't do that." You have to work this process over and over because we are all slow to learn. But if you are patient, pretty soon you'll get into a habit and the habit becomes a routine and instead of living in a rut, you will define a new reality. You will be redeeming the time, maximizing your life.

Prayer

Father, we thank you for your wisdom. We thank you for your truth that sets us free from living in the rut of our daily routines. We thank you for the time you give us. Teach us to redeem the time so that we might know your will in reality, just as our Lord Jesus did. Your will may be for us to spend two hours with a grandchild instead of leading a Bible class or impressing other people with our credentials. What a sense of eternity we get when we know that we are right where You want us to be, even by a pond fishing with a six year old son. Lord, teach us to maximize our time and make our journey worthy of our destination. In Christ's name, Amen.

CHAPTER 11

Knowing Your Priest

For we do not have a high priest who is not able of sympathizing with our weaknesses, but one who has been tempted in every way as we are, yet without sin. Therefore let us approach the throne of grace confidently to receive mercy and find grace whenever we need help.
HEBREWS 4:15–16

Moving From Milk to Meat

In Hebrews 5, the writer has been talking about Jesus as a Priest in the order of Melchizedek. This is not a topic that we hear discussed everyday and it can be difficult to deal with. There are some spiritual truths that are hard to explain and also hard to understand. They are not impossible to understand, just hard. As teachers, we try to illustrate and explain these truths, but they are difficult. So he says,

> 1 About this we have much to say, and it is hard to explain, since you have become dull of hearing. 12 For though by this time you ought to be teachers, you need someone to teach you again the basic principles of the oracles of God. You need milk, not solid food, 13 for everyone who lives on

milk is unskilled in the word of righteousness, since he is a child. 14 But solid food is for the mature, for those who have their powers of discernment trained by constant practice to distinguish good from evil.   Hebrews 5:11–14

Part of the problem with these believers is that they had become "dull of hearing." They weren't born dull of hearing; they had become that way. As Christians they had progressively lived so near the railroad track, so to speak, that they didn't hear the trains anymore. You can do that as a Christian. You can get so deep into a rut of Christian life that you just don't hear God anymore. He warns us all not to get that way—there are always many more things we need to learn.

Now look at what he says in verse 12: "By this time you ought to be teachers." Not every Christian has the gift of teaching, but everybody teaches. Some of you have taught your children how to eat and how to tie shoes. You may teach people at your office how to use the copier. We all teach in one way or another. When you learn spiritual truths and how to apply them to your own life, you can teach others the same. We should all be able to teach what we know. Here, the writer implies that after a certain amount of time, every Christian should be able to teach the "basic principles" of God's Word. We might call these the ABCs of spiritual truth.

Now instead of being teachers and growing, this group of Christians had stagnated. They actually needed someone to go back teach them their ABCs again. That's not good. Using another word picture, he says they had gone back to needing "milk" because they could not handle "meat"—solid food. Milk is great if you are a baby, but you can't stay there, you can't grow only drinking milk.

I remember raising our kids and they all started on the bottle, the milk. Pretty soon, they take the next step up and it's that ground up, mashed up stuff—the apricots, squash, oatmeal and mashed bananas—no salt or sugar. I've tasted that stuff and it is terrible. Jeannie would fill the little baby spoon and say, "Mmmmmmmmmm". She would put it in and they would spit it out. But then they would get used to it and then they would be saying, "Mmmmmmmmmmmm," eating as fast as we could put it in. I would sit there thinking, "That's not food. Kid, you have no idea what's waiting for you." But they would eat it. They would eat whatever we put in front of them. Then we would start slipping some stuff in—real peas, real food. Their eyes would light up, "Where's this been all my life?"

Then you reach the stage where they want to feed themselves. When they first start feeding themselves eating is very mechanical—they had to really concentrate on everything they were doing. We gave them a little spoon and they'd rake things all around. Every fourth bite went in the mouth and most everything else went on the floor. But that stage doesn't last very long. If you were to watch my children now, they can eat and never look down! It's become an unconscious thing. They don't miss any more. What was once a very mechanical exercise has now become just motionless; it just flows.

The Christian life ought to be that way. First, it's mechanical. We have to slow down. We work on the ABCs. We work on the basic principles. That's the milk. Now we have to be weaned off the milk and move on to the "mush"—the pablum. Then little by little we move on to the solid food. As our digestive system grows, we can eat and digest it all. We learn how to use a knife and fork and now we are really going. Once you have moved on to the "meat"—the solid food—you don't want to go back to the "milk" or the "mush."

Unfortunately there are Christians who go back to the "milk" or who never grown out of that stage. You know what the "milk" is?—"Jesus loves me, this I know for the Bible tells me so." Milk is, "Now I lay me down to sleep, I pray the Lord my soul to keep…" as you fall asleep and don't know whether you finished it. That's milk. Everybody starts there but you don't want to stay there.

The writer tells us, "for everyone who lives on milk is unskilled in the word of righteousness, since he is a child." This is what I call a "baby Christian." A "baby Christian" is someone who is "unskilled in the word of righteousness"—the Bible. We tend to think that a person's spiritual maturity is measured by how many years they have been in church, and the offices they have held and the accolades they have received. The Bible doesn't teach that. It says that everyone that is unskilled in the word of God is a baby, a child spiritually speaking.

Finally, the writer says, "But solid food is for the mature, for those who have their powers of discernment trained by constant practice to distinguish good from evil." That ought to be the definition of spiritual maturity. A mature Christian can handle the "meat"—they know the Word of God, even the difficult things, and they have trained their discernment through constant practice. This means they have heard the Word, they have digested the Word and they have learned to apply the Word to their lives. In doing this, they know the difference between "Good and Evil." Because they know God's Word, His truth, it is obvious to them what's right and what's wrong. That's the spiritually mature person.

I encourage you to think about where you are with God. Am I a "milk Christian"? Or am I a "meat Christian"? He says that meat belongs to those that are mature. I would challenge you to think about this.

Jesus: A Priest in the Order of Melchizedek

Now I have started with all of that because I want us to talk about this "meat truth" that the writer of Hebrews was discussing in chapter 5. There he talks about Jesus as "a High Priest after the order of Melchizedek." You might say, "So what?" What I want to show you is that if you understand that Jesus is a priest in the order of Melchizedek, it will change your life. This is meat, not milk.

When God established the priesthood in Israel, He gave it to the family of Aaron. So all of the "official" priests were the sons and grandsons of Aaron. Jesus however, is not in the line of Aaron and yet He is THE High Priest. How can that be? The writer tells us it is because He is in the order of Melchizedek—a Priest who served in the time of Abraham, many years before God established Israel's priesthood through Aaron. Once Aaron came on the scene with Moses, the Lord said that all of the priesthood would come from Aaron's descendants.

The writer then explains to us that Jesus is a far better priest because He never dies; He serves as a priest forever (Hebrews 7:17, 21, 25). The Aaronic priests, from the old way, died and so could never serve as a priest forever (Hebrews 7:23). Every year, Aaron and all of his descendants had to go *once* into the Holy of Holies and offer up the animal sacrifices but these sacrifices could never take away sin, they merely "covered" it (Hebrews 9:7; 10:4, 11). Jesus went once into the Heavenly Tabernacle to give one sacrifice for sin for all time (Hebrews 7:27; 9:12, 26; 10:10). Aaron and all his descendants practiced their priesthood on earth; Jesus practices His in heaven (Hebrews 9:11-14, 24). Aaron offered the blood of animals; Jesus offered His own blood (Hebrews 9:12-14). The Aaronic priest had to buy a sacrifice; Jesus was both Priest and Sacrifice (Hebrews 10:11-12). Now think about this verse for a minute:

> Now According to [The old way of the Law], gifts and sacrifices are offered that cannot perfect the conscience of the worshiper, ... 9:11 But when Christ appeared as a High Priest of the good things that have come, ... 9:12 He entered once for all into the Holy Place, not by means of the blood of goats and calves but by means of His own blood, thus securing eternal redemption. 9:13 For if the blood of goats and bulls, and the sprinkling of defiled persons with the ashes of a heifer, sanctify for the purification of the flesh, 9:14 how much more will the blood of Christ, who through the eternal Spirit offered Himself without blemish to God, purify our conscience from dead works to serve the living God.
>
> Hebrews 9:9–14

The blood of an animal could never, ever clear your conscience. That's why you will not find the Old Testament talking about people having their consciences cleared. If you committed a sin under the Law of Moses and brought the appropriate offering, it "covered" that sin. When you sinned again, you needed another sacrifice. Now, the blood of Christ cleanses us so that we can move on. We have a Superior Priest, who has offered Superior Blood in a Superior Place performing a Superior Work. What I want share with you now is that He wants us to come to Him. The doors are always open and He wants us to come.

What is Jesus Doing Right Now?

Jesus Christ functions in three offices: He is a prophet, He is a Priest and He is a King. When He became incarnate, when He came into our world as a human, He came to fill the office of a prophet. He would teach and say, "Now I say to you ...," that is how a prophet functions. Jesus also offered Israel the Kingdom during His earthly ministry, but they rejected Him as King. Even though many in the nation had come to believe in Him, the national leaders swayed the crowds so that they rejected Jesus. Jesus will return as The King to set up His kingdom, but that is yet future.

It is good to understand what Jesus did when He was on the earth and it's good to study eschatology—what He will do in the future. What I'd really like to concentrate on here is what Jesus is doing right now. That brings us to His third office.

Right now Jesus Christ is at the right hand of the Father and He is functioning as The High Priest. He is a High Priest for all people. He is the High Priest of anyone who comes to know Him as their personal Lord and Savior. He is sitting at the right hand of His Father not because He is tired, or because He is indifferent; He is sitting because He has accomplished what the Father sent Him to do. That's why He is sitting.

Everything in this world that is over your head is already under His feet. That's why every time you are tempted to panic, you just need to look up and realize that Jesus is not biting his nails, He is not leaning forward in his seat wondering what terrible thing might happen here in Memphis or anywhere in the world. He doesn't wait for USA Today or turn on the morning news. His word for you and me today as our High Priest is "Just remember, until you see Me panic, don't you panic. *And you'll never see Me panic.*"

I know the condition the world is getting into. Dark days seem to get darker. Trends seem to spiral downward. If you just focus on what's happening among the people here on the earth, you'll probably get pessimistic. We need to realize that nothing ever happens that isn't already under His feet. He's still seated. He isn't panicked. He isn't fretting.

Two thousand years ago, God made a statement when He nailed Jesus to that Cross and revealed the truth to us. The truth is we all need a Savior and God has provided that Savior in Jesus. The question is, "What are you going to do about it?" When people ask me, "What's God been doing the last two thousand years?" I always say, "He's waiting to see how you and I respond to His Son!" He is patiently waiting, but there will come a day when God will say, "That's enough." For two thousand years men have progressively denied, rejected and explained away Christ. They've taken on alternatives. Now God has been patient, but there will come an end and He will move on to finish things up. He is not asleep, He is not dead, but He is waiting.

Jesus Is Your High Priest

"For we do not have a High Priest incapable of sympathizing with our weaknesses, but one who has been tempted in every way just as we are, yet without sin. Therefore let us boldly approach the throne of grace to receive mercy and find grace whenever we need help."   Hebrews 4:15–16

Jesus is functioning in His office as a priest right now and He is your High Priest. We are told that we do not have a High Priest who cannot sympathize with our weaknesses. When you come to Christ and talk to him about family squabbles, about issues, it isn't like he can't understand. He was on this earth, He had a body just like yours and mine. He grew up with a family with half-brothers and half-sisters. The Gospels indicate that He was a carpenter by trade and so we can assume that He worked in His father's shop. He was the fellow you would call to put an addition on your house. For many years of His life, He worked with His hands in the little town of Nazareth.

When His "earthly father" died (and it seems that Joseph may have died by the time Jesus was twenty or so), being the eldest son, He would have assumed the headship of the house. Mary looked to Him. He knew what it was to be the breadwinner and to support a family. From what we can glean from the Gospels, it seems His family was poor, as were most people in His times. Imagine Him trying to get enough money because His half brothers wanted to get those newest Nike sandals! And the half sisters always needed new robes—styles change you know!

He knew what it was to live with others and the griping, complaining, arguing, and hassling that goes along with being part of family. He grew up through His teens and twenties and lived into His thirties. It was essential for Him to go through that exercise so that He can sympathize with us. He had to experience human life so that when you and I come to Him with a common, garden variety, every day problem of life that pulls us down, He doesn't say, "I can't relate. I don't understand what you're talking about." That is not the kind of High Priest we have.

The writer of Hebrews tells us that as our High Priest Jesus can sympathize with us. Why? Because He was tempted in all the ways that you and I are tempted, yet He didn't sin. When it says that He was tempted in all ways like us, it doesn't mean He was tempted with every specific kind of sin we are tempted with: Jesus was never tempted to waste hours watching soap operas! And you have never been tempted to turn stones into bread because you can't do that anyway. So when it says, "He was tempted in every way as we are," what does that really mean?

Three Areas of Temptation

"For all that is in the world—the desires of the flesh and the desires of the eyes and pride of life—is not from the Father but is from the world." (1 John 2:16)

In his first letter, John helps us with the answer to that question. All temptation falls into one of three broad categories: the desires of flesh, the desires of the eyes and the pride of life.

When Satan came to Jesus and tempted Him to turn the stones into bread, that was a temptation of the desires of the flesh. Jesus was hungry, He needed to eat and so Satan tempted Him.

Satan took Jesus up on a high place and showed Him all the kingdoms of the earth in flash. He then promised Jesus all the kingdoms of the earth if He would just fall down and worship the Devil. That was a temptation in the area of the desires of the eyes—everything Jesus had just seen could be His if He just bowed down. Jesus didn't deny that the Kingdom were under Satan's power because Satan is the Prince of this present age. But Jesus would not worship the Devil, only His Father alone.

Then Satan said to Him, "You need to prove that you are the Messiah. If you will cast yourself off the pinnacle of the temple, the Scriptures say that the angels have been given charge over you, to protect you—they'll catch you." That was a temptation in area of the pride of life.

Jesus successfully navigated all three of these temptations. He was tempted in all areas yet He did not sin. Pay attention to that last idea there: He was tempted, but He did not sin. He's no ordinary priest. We have a lot of earthly priests, but there has never been a priest in the history of humanity that didn't sin. We have a High Priest that while He identifies with all our temptations, He did not sin.

What I'm saying is Jesus can be approached because He has been through all the difficulties that life in this present world has to offer: He grew up in poverty, He grew up working with His hands, He grew up with a family who didn't even believe in Him at first, He lived in a society that was a work-a-day, "blue collar" world. He understands who we are and what we are going through. We can come to Him because He is sympathetic to us.

Come Boldly Before Him

Now back in verse 16 of Hebrews 4 it says, "Therefore, let us boldly approach the throne of Joy." It doesn't just say, "come" it says come boldly. We do not approach God arrogantly, but we do come boldly in light of all that He has done for us.

I used to envision approaching the throne room of the King of kings and Lord of lords and there stand these huge closed doors. I knew that I was a child of God, but I saw myself standing out there in the "foyer" to the throne room while inside, Jesus was sitting at the right hand of His Father. Of course, Satan is always whispering, "You can't go in there. Look at our life. Look at the condition of your life. You can't go in there. Not now, you've got to get some things straightened up." I am sure some of you probably envision things this way. So you stand out in the foyer and all the time Jesus is sitting there just waiting for you.

But Jesus is a sympathetic High Priest. He wants you to come as His child just as you are. He understands the attacks of Satan. He understands all the pressures of life. He understands that you sin. Now He has provided a way of escape through temptation and He will challenge you to resist and grow in grace. But even in your failure, you are never denied access to His presence!

Sometimes when I pray with other Christians, they'll say, "Why don't you just pray?" I can immediately sense that they are saying, "Well you go on through the doors. I'll wait out here in the foyer." I want to say, "Why should I get to go in there any more than you! I'm just a dirty as you are. Why don't we both go? I am no more His child than you are. Why should you be denied access to Him?"

Receive His Mercy in Your Time of Need

Mercy is something that we don't deserve but we desperately need. Whenever someone is cold busted in a crime and has no defense—zero defense—what is the common practice? They throw themselves on the mercy of the court. Now look at the end of the Hebrews 4:16: "Therefore let us boldly approach the throne of grace to receive mercy and find grace whenever we need help." We come boldly to Jesus because we need mercy, we need help in our time of need. When do you need Him most? When you have no defense. And that is often the one time we won't go to Him.

The person who wants mercy is a person who doesn't want justice. When you stand in Jesus' presence, He knows everything that is going on with you. In Jesus, you have a High Priest that says, "I would love to see you when you're at your worst." You know why? Because you can't appreciate mercy until you have no defense. You cannot experience His grace and mercy until you come through those doors in prayer, into His presence and lift your eyes to His, and say from your heart, "I'm dead guilty. I rebelled. I did it. I am totally guilty." That's when a child of God experiences the mercy and grace that is available to every one of us.

Imagine Jesus saying to you, "Where are your accusers?" just as He said to the woman taken in adultery. Satan can accuse you, but He cannot convict or condemn: you are in the presence of The Justifier. Imagine Jesus saying to you, "You are forgiven. Go and sin no more. It is not necessary for you to be doing this." We come out of that room with a grin on our face, eyes aglow. You don't have to wait until you get to heaven to experience His mercy and grace

It must grieve the Father's heart that there are many who don't even come to the foyer of the throne room. I can just visualize those who are in the foyer pushing one another, "You go see what kind of mood He's in …" That's not what Father God wants of us. He says that we ought to come boldly. You don't march in arrogantly. You come in confidently and stand before Him saying, "Lord, I have two options. I can stay out there in the foyer and not experience your mercy and grace or I can come in here and get both." Every moment we stay out there in the foyer is a moment we could be spending in His presence because the facts are not going to change. If I stay out there an hour, two hours or ten days it still doesn't change the fact that I'm still dead guilty. I might as well go in quickly and take full responsibility. It is only when you take full responsibility that you can ever experience full pardon.

God tells us that we are to come in our time of need. If He's offering you that proposition, you can come when you need mercy, not justice. When do you most need mercy? It's when you are most sinful. That's when you need to come. He says, "Why don't my children come to me?" Why don't they come?" He says, "Since you have such a great High Priest in my son, why don't you appeal to Him? Why don't you take advantage of what He is offering you?"

I encourage you to consider that you have a High Priest, seated at the right hand of the Father, just waiting for those doors to swing open and for the dirtiest, guilt ridden, defenseless child of God to come and stand in His presence and say, "Father, I have sinned." Then you will experience the sweetest smile, the tenderest compassion— grace and mercy beyond any words to describe. You will walk out and when people say, "Why are you grinning?" You'll say, "I've been with my High Priest."

Prayer

Father, we thank you for the truth that sets us free from condemnation and shame. We thank you for our Lord Jesus who is such a faithful and sympathetic High Priest. We are so overjoyed that we can come into your presence boldly—not flippantly, not disrespectfully—but reverently and with a sincere heart. We thank you that we can claim Christ's sacrifice, His holiness, and His mercy. We thank you that we have received a cleansing in Him that even purifies our consciences. We thank you that you have removed our sins from us and that you will remember them no more. I pray that those who have never know this before will begin to discover what a great High Priest they have in Jesus. Thank you for your goodness to each of us in Christ. Amen.

CHAPTER 12

Victory Over Death

Now when this perishable puts on the imperishable,
and this mortal puts on immortality,
then the saying that is written will happen,
"Death has been swallowed up in victory!
Where, O death, is your victory?
Where, O death, is your sting?"
1 CORINTHIANS 15:54–55

Some years back, I led a young lady to the Lord and she had one of those "alka-seltzer" personalities. Soon after she became a Christian she was just insatiable to know more about Christ. It wasn't long after that she was diagnosed with Lymphoma. She was in her twenties. When the diagnosis came, we began to work with her to encourage her since she was such a new Christian. Things got bad, she had to go through a lot of chemotherapy, but in all this she had a tremendous spirit and she really trusted the Lord.

Then excitement came when we got the good news that the cancer went into remission. There was celebration. It looked like some real progress was being made. But after a while the heartache came; the cancer had returned and it was worse. More chemo, more treatments. Things just bottomed out.

In the middle of this, we found out that she was pregnant. She and her husband had been trying for a long time to have a child. But they eventually had to take the child—it was a little boy; they had wanted a little boy. So there was more heartache. As things moved along, she realized that it didn't look like she would survive the cancer. She asked me then to come by her house and teach her about heaven. She was bedridden at that time and could not even hold her own Bible. I would go to her house and teach her about heaven.

It was at that time that I began to really wrestle for the first time in my life with Heaven as a reality. I had always believed in Heaven, but I had never had to face the reality of it. Now I was watching someone die daily. As I would explain to her what the Scriptures said about heaven, about going to be there with the Lord, her eyes would light up and there would be a glow across her face. I was the one actually receiving the blessing.

I was with her in the hospital holding her hand the night she died. I was even telling her to go ahead, to move on. I was tired of watching her heave for one more breath. We had been doing that for weeks around the clock. I kept saying, "It's OK, go ahead and go." Her husband was in the chapel praying when I had to go get him. She had already gone to be with the Lord. My experience with my dear friends in this was the trigger that made me want to find out more about what happens at death and more about Heaven.

Since then, I have had the joy and the pain of carrying many of my friends, as a pallbearer, to their graves. I have learned that the older we get the more funerals we have to attend. A lot of my friends have gone to be with the Lord. So I have wanted to learn all I can about this topic.

What is Death?

First of all, I want to lay out a good biblical definition of death. The Bible never speaks about death as extinction or annihilation or cessation. It does not present the idea that when life is over, it is just over. Death, in all of its forms, is simply separation. The Bible talks about three types of death and I want go over those briefly now.

The first is spiritual death and that is where we are separated from the life of God. This is the first type of death that Adam introduced and experienced in the Garden when he rebelled. As we have already discussed, all of us were born into this situation. Our human parents passed on their physical life to us, but they were not able to transmit spiritual life. So we were born physically alive, yet spiritually dead. This is why Jesus said, "You must be born again!" (John 3:3). He also says, "I have come that you may have life" (John 10:10). Who needs life? Dead people need life and Jesus has come to restore us to spiritual life.

The second form of death is physical death and that is simply the separation of our spiritual selves from our physical bodies—the separation of the immaterial part of us from the material part. At this point it is important for you to remember that your personality is found in the immaterial, spiritual part of you. So when we bury someone, we are placing the physical remains in the ground but the immaterial part does not cease to exist. Your body is no longer functioning, but you are still conscious, you are still thinking, you still feel—you have all the characteristics of your personality and that part of you has been separated from your physical body.

The final form of death that the Bible talks about is eternal death, the second death, and it is the separation from the presence of God forever. In Revelation 20 we get a glimpse of this at the Great White Throne Judgment. All of the wicked dead are raised—all those who died outside of God's salvation—and are cast into the Lake of Fire, away from the presence of God. So the second death is that death that is final and cemented forever for those who are not saved.

Destroying the Devil

When Jesus entered into our world, He came as a human, He took on a physical body just like you and I have. Part of the reason for this, as the writer of Hebrews tells us, is so that He might destroy the Devil, the one who held the power of death up to that point:

Since therefore the children share in flesh and blood, [Christ] Himself likewise partook of the same things, that through death He might destroy the one who has the power of death, that is, the Devil, and deliver all those who through fear of death were subject to lifelong slavery.   Hebrews 2:14-15

As we said, when Adam fell, he introduced death into the human experience. The one who held the power of death from that time on was Satan, or the Devil, as the writer calls him here. So one of the reasons that Jesus came as a human to die on the Cross and then be physically resurrected from the dead was to destroy the Devil who held the power of death.

From the fall of Adam until the death, burial and resurrection of Jesus, Satan used his power over death to enslave people in fear. That is why the writer of Hebrews says that Jesus is able to deliver us from our fear of death and the slavery that goes along with it. When you and I think about death, we don't have to be afraid. Instead there is victory for us because of what Christ has already accomplished for us.

Now the Old Testament saints lived with the fear of death and rightly so. During that time, the Devil used the fear of death to keep men and women enslaved. Where the writer says "he who has the power of death" seems to imply that the Devil had the authority to administer death before Christ. The Rabbis themselves had talked about the Devil as the "angel of death." Now that Christ has come, the Devil's ability to enslave us with that fear of death has been destroyed.

Now even when the Devil held the power of death and could administer death, he could not determine someone's eternal destination. In Old Testament times, God had not revealed as much about death and what happens after death as He did after Jesus had come. They understood that when someone died they would go to the grave, the place of the dead. In your Bible, you will see the word "sheol" in the Old Testament and that is just referring generally to the place of the dead. They viewed this in a more literal way and since people were buried in the ground or in caves or tombs in the earth. When you died you went down into sheol.

They also understood that there were two "sides" of sheol: one for the righteous and one for the wicked. You might have already noticed that the Old Testament doesn't talk about "going to heaven." When a righteous person dies, they would say, "he was gathered to his people" as with Abraham (Genesis 25:8) or Jacob (Genesis 49:29). You will also see the phrase, "he was gathered to his fathers" (Judges 2:10, 2 Kings 22:20). By the time of Jesus, they would talk about the righteous being taken to the "Bosom of Abraham"—he was the father of the nation of Israel and so all the righteous who had followed in his footsteps of faith would be gathered to him in death. Later, Christians began talking about going to Heaven because they knew that Jesus was there and at their physical death, they would go to be with Him.

Now the unrighteous, or wicked dead—those who died outside of God's salvation were gathered to a very different place. This place comes to be known as "hades" (the Greek term from which we get the word "hell") by New Testament times, but in the Hebrew Scriptures it is sometimes referred to as "the pit" (Ezekiel 28:8). There is a lot more we can say about this, but we want to focus on what happens to believers at the point of death.

When Jesus comes and begins to teach, He reveals much more about death and what happens after. You will remember His story of the rich man and Lazarus in Luke 16:19-31 where Lazarus, the poor beggar, is in "Abraham's Bosom" and the rich man is in torment in Hades, or Hell. There was a great gulf separating them that neither could pass. The rich man could see Lazarus and pleaded with Abraham to let Lazarus quench his thirst and then go back to the land of the living and warn his brothers. Father Abraham refused his requests however. You are probably familiar with that story, if not, take the time to read it through very carefully.

What I want you to understand is that Jesus indicates that both Lazarus and the rich man are conscious in their post death situations: one in comfort, one in torment. The rich man can think and reason—he is certainly not annihilated. He knows who

Abraham is; He knows who Lazarus is. He knows the dire situation his brothers are in.

There are no Atheists in Hell, no agnostics and no liberals because at that point, they all know the truth! The tragedy however is that it is too late. There are even some evangelists there: this rich man wants to send Lazarus back from the dead to warn his brothers because surely they would listen to someone who had come back from the dead. Abraham says, "If they do not hear Moses and the Prophets, neither will they be convinced if someone should rise from the dead!" (Luke 16:31).

Based on the teaching of Jesus and later Paul and the other New Testament writers, we can understand that when someone dies and their body goes in the ground, their immaterial part—their spirit or soul—continues on thinking, feeling, remembering. Death is not "soul sleep" as some have postulated and it is not a cessation or annihilation. Jesus clearly teaches that none of these views are true.

How Did Jesus Change Everything?

We need to spend some time now understanding what happened with Jesus' death, burial, resurrection and ascension because all of this changed the way God deals with those who die in faith. As we know, Jesus shed His blood on the Cross to take away our sins. Jesus' sacrifice of Himself provided an entirely new sacrifice that was different from any other sacrifice ever given.

In the times of the Old Testament, God introduced animal sacrifices in order to cover over sins, for "without the shedding of blood there can be no forgiveness of sin" (Hebrews 9:22). In the Garden of Eden after the Fall, God shed the blood of two innocent animals to make a covering for Adam and Eve's sin (Genesis 3:21). All of the animal sacrifice only covered over sin. Now what God also revealed was that although animal blood was sufficient to keep you out of hell, it was not enough to get you into Heaven—into the very presence of God: "For it is impossible for the blood of bulls and goats to take away sins" (Hebrews 10:4).

When Jesus came to offer Himself as a sacrifice, His blood did not merely cover sins, but actually took sins away. You will remember how John the Baptist described Jesus: "Behold, the Lamb of God, who takes away the sin of the world!" (John 1:29). John also says later, "You know that He [Jesus] appeared in order to take away sins, and in Him there is no sin" (1 John 3:5). The truth that Jesus has actually taken our sins away is crucial to understanding what happens when someone in Christ dies.

On the day of Jesus' crucifixion, around three in the afternoon Jesus gave up His life as He said, "Father, into your hands I commit my spirit" (Luke 23:46). What happened then? His spirit—His immaterial part—separated from His physical body. Joseph of Arimathea and Nicodemus took His body from the cross, prepared it for burial and then placed it in a tomb. Joseph probably had no idea that he would be getting his tomb back in three days! So as Jesus' body was into the tomb, His spirit—His personality—went to the Father.

You will also remember that Jesus said to the thief on the Cross, "Today, you will be with me in Paradise" (Luke 23:43). Paradise was another word that the Jewish people used to talk about the place of the righteous dead. At the time of Jesus, there would have been many saints from the Old Testament era already there in Abraham's Bosom or Paradise. What were they doing? They were awaiting the day for the Messiah to come and open up the way fully into Heaven—the very presence of God. They were awaiting the day of their final redemption.

You may remember Simeon who had been present when Jesus was brought to the Temple as a baby to be dedicated to the Lord (Luke 2:22-35). Simeon was a devout man who had been waiting for the salvation of Israel to come. He got to see and hold Jesus and He blessed God because the Lord revealed to him that this baby was the Messiah—the one who would bring salvation for all. The day Simeon died and was gathered to his people in Abraham's bosom, in Paradise—can you imagine him telling them, "I have seen the

Savior! I held Him! He is on the earth!" You can imagine all those saints getting excited.

During Jesus' lifetime there were several people who died and were gathered to Paradise who would have told the people all that was going on. Joseph, Jesus' earthly "father" would have told them, "Yes, He has arrived. He was conceived of the Holy Spirit to my wife Mary just as the Scriptures foretold." You can imagine John the Baptist showing up giving them his report: "He is healing the sick, giving sight to the blind, raising the dead." You can imagine all those souls getting very excited about what might happen next?

Now imagine late on the day of His crucifixion, Jesus himself shows up there in Paradise with the thief on His arm. They might have been a little surprised to see the kind of company that the Savior was keeping. But He only hangs out with bad company because those are the only people who need a Savior. That's how He met me and how He met you.

Now Jesus was there in Paradise Friday night, all day Saturday and into the early morning hours of Sunday morning. You can imagine that He was probably answering a million questions. Then on the third day, on Sunday morning, His Spirit left paradise and went back to the Tomb where it was united to His body again. But it was not His old body; it was His resurrection body. At that point, some really interesting things happened.

Jesus first appeared to Mary who was looking for His body at the tomb. She did not recognize Him at first, and so Jesus revealed Himself to her (see John 20:15–18). When she understands that it is Jesus, He says to her, *"Don't cling to Me, for I have not yet ascended to my Father."* What does that mean? The writer of Hebrews helps us to understand Jesus' statement where he says,

> Thus it was necessary for the copies of the heavenly things to be purified with these rites (animal Sacrifices), but the heavenly things themselves with better sacrifices than these. For Christ has entered, not into holy places made with hands (the earthly temple), which are copies of the true things, but

into heaven itself, now to appear in the presence of God on our behalf. Nor was it to offer Himself repeatedly, as the high priest enters the holy places every year with blood not His own, for then He would have had to suffer repeatedly since the foundation of the world. But as it is, He has appeared once for all at the end of the ages to put away sin by the sacrifice of Himself.   Hebrews 9:23–26

You see Jesus entered into the Heavenly Temple on the day of His resurrection and offered up His blood to make a cleansing for sin, for all people, for all time. That day, Jesus blood was offered up in the True Temple in Heaven not to merely cover our sins, as the animal sacrifices had done, but to actually pay the debt of our sins and therefore remove their defilement and guilt.

I believe that I can make the case biblically that Satan, before he rebelled and fell, was the Anointed Cherub and functioned as the Angelic high priest in Heaven (see Ezekiel 28:14). When he and a third of the angels rebelled, he lost his role as Priest and his sin would have desecrated the Heavenly Temple. When Jesus comes offering His blood, the Temple is cleansed and He also takes the role of High Priest of Heaven itself.

After Jesus had offered His sacrifice in the Heavenly Temple He came back to earth for forty days when He taught the disciples and prepared them for the reality that He would be ascending back into Heaven and leaving His ministry to carry on with them. Then on the day of His ascension, Paul gives us some insight into what happened: "Therefore it says, 'When He [Christ] ascended on high He led a host of captives, and He gave gifts to men'" (Ephesians 4:8). Who were these "captives" that Paul is referring to here? These are the Old Testament saints that had been waiting in Abraham's Bosom.

So it seems that Christ went back to Paradise, to Abraham's bosom, in His resurrected body to lead those Old Testament saints into Heaven itself through the new way that He had opened for them. You can imagine them asking, "When are we going to get our resurrection bodies?" Jesus would have said, "Not yet, but I have overcome death—you see I have the keys of death and even Hell ..." In Revelation 1:18 we see that Jesus now has those keys to death. Remember He has destroyed the Devil who had the power of death and so now Jesus Himself has the keys to death.

Until the offering of the sacrifice of Christ, the way into the Heavenly Temple itself had not been opened. All those animal sacrifices only covered sin, but they could not bring actual cleansing—the removal, the taking away of sins. Only Jesus' blood could do that. The animal blood, offered in faith, could cover your sins and get you as far as Paradise, but no further. When Jesus came, offering His blood, He opened the doors to Heaven itself:

> Since therefore, brothers and sisters, we have confidence to enter the Holy Place (Heaven itself) by the blood of Jesus, by a new and living way which He inaugurated for us through the veil, that is, His flesh, and since we have a great priest over the house of God, let us draw near with a sincere heart in full assurance of faith, having our hearts sprinkled clean from an evil conscience and our bodies washed with pure water.
>
> Hebrews 10:18–22

After The Ascension

Now after Jesus' ascension back into Heaven, everyone who dies "in Christ" goes directly into His presence. Paul tells us that to be absent from the body is to be present, at home, with the Lord (see 1 Corinthians 5:6-8). So no one who dies "in Christ" now goes to Abraham's Bosom or any other holding place, but directly to the presence of Christ who is at the right hand of the Father.

Right now, Jesus holds the keys to death and hell (Revelation 1:8). What does that mean for us who are in Christ? It means that death should hold no fear for us. Satan no longer has the power to administer and use death to keep us scared to death. The minute our spirit—the immaterial part of us—separates from our physical body at the point of physical death, our personality is immediately in the presence of Jesus. Once you are spiritually "Alive in Christ," you are alive forever. Your physical death is not the end, it is just the time that you let go of your physical body in order to be with Christ. How comforting is that?

We all have a natural apprehension about things that we have not ever experienced. That is especially true of death. But if we trust what the Scriptures tell us about death, we can enter into that time realizing that it will actually be wonderful. Before the nurse will be able to pull the sheet over your head, before anybody can take your final pulse, before anyone says to your family, "I am sorry..." in less time than it takes for light to bounce off your eye, you will be present with the Lord. You will not feel the cold or dark of the grave. You will not feel alone, you will not be abandoned.

It is not necessarily a lack of faith or trust to have some apprehension about death. What is important is that you let you apprehension be overcome by the Truth. If you know the Truth, the Truth will set you free. The Truth is that Christ has overcome death, He has the keys to death and so He administers death now. He died for you and He is waiting to welcome you into His presence. Now it is going to cost you something to go be with Him; it will cost you your physical body. In your present body you cannot see God. You will have to turn loose of your body; I will have to turn loose of my body to go to Him.

I will have to shed this "tent," this "earthly tabernacle" of my body in order to be with Christ. But my "tent" is already 52 years old, its dying day by day, wrinkling, sagging, losing it sight, losing its memory, stumbling around a lot, getting older every day. Toward the end of His life, Paul realized his earthly tent was getting ready to be "folded up." For some of you, your tent is close to being "folded up" as well! But the longer we wear this "tent" the more it is going to be worn out. We shouldn't let this worry us too much or cause us to fear because it just means that we are moving closer to the time when we will be with the Lord.

What is the Resurrection?

Right now, the only human who has a resurrected body is Jesus. He is the "firstfruits" of the resurrection:

> But now Christ has been raised from the dead, the firstfruits of those who are asleep. For since by a man came death, by a man also came the resurrection of the dead. For as in Adam all die, so also in Christ all shall be made alive. But each in his own order: Christ the firstfruits, after that those who are Christ's at His coming, then comes the end, when He delivers up the kingdom to the God and Father, when He has abolished all rule and all authority and power.
>
>   1 Corinthians 15:20–24

Everyone who has died in faith, who is now in Heaven, does not yet have a resurrection body. They are all present with Christ, but they do not yet have their new bodies. They are not flying around like ghosts, nor or they in some kind of soul sleep, as we have seen they are conscious and active. But I imagine them all looking at Christ with His resurrected, glorified body saying, "When are we going to get ours?" "Not yet," Jesus says, "but soon."

Jesus was the "first fruits" of the resurrection and there will not be another resurrection until His return to Earth in the last days. At His appearing toward the end of this present age, all those who belong to Him will be instantaneously transformed:

> "Behold! I tell you a mystery. We shall not all sleep, but we shall all be changed, in a moment, in the twinkling of an eye, at the last trumpet. For the trumpet will sound, and the dead will be raised imperishable, and we shall be changed. For this perishable body must put on the imperishable, and this mortal body must put on immortality. When the perishable puts on the imperishable, and the mortal puts on immortality, then shall come to pass the saying that is written: *Death is swallowed up in victory*." 1 Corinthians 15:51–54

Your present body is not fit to live in eternity. But one day, at the resurrection, you and I will be given new, glorified bodies—like the body Jesus has right now—and then we will be fit for eternity. That new body will not wear out, it will not get old, or tired, or wrinkled. Can you imagine that? At our physical death, we will have to let go of our present bodies, but we know that we have a new, better version coming.

Freed from the Fear of Death

I want you to know that if you are a believer, if you are "in Christ" you really should have no reason to fear death. I want you to know that when you die, your passing into the presence of Christ will not be a traumatic, scary experience. The Bible says it is like falling asleep. You don't realize the exact moment you fall asleep at night, but you do remember the last time you looked at the clock. Just like when you wake up, unless someone wakes you with start, it usually happens in degrees; we slip into sleep and we slip out.

At the point of your death, when your spirit separates from your body, you are not going to experience a great turmoil. You might experience this world fading away the same way all the chaos and noise of traffic disappears as you roll up your car window. The turmoil of this world will slip away from you. I believe there is going to be such peace and serenity as you enter the presence of Jesus and meet Him personally.

I have often imagined that we will have time to look on His face, touch His hands and feet where the nail prints are, and have the opportunity to thank Him, praise Him for all He has done for us. I am looking forward to that day. I have said it to Him many times already, but I am looking forward to the day I can look in His eyes and say it to Him face to face. Then we will have millions of years to meet everybody else and talk with them. I want to go see Adam; I have a lot of questions for him.

So when it comes to your time, or the time of a loved one, I want you to know that "In Christ" to be absent from your body is to be present with the Lord. When I come to my time, whether they tell me cancer has taken my body or old age or whatever it may be, I want to say to the Lord, "Listen if I have to shed this tabernacle of my body, this cocoon, in order to get into your presence, I'm happy to give it up; its wearing out anyway!"

Death does not intimidate me because Christ has come and opened the way into Heaven before me. He has defeated the Devil and He has the keys of death. He has never done anything but good for me, never any harm, therefore I am not afraid. I know that I am not going into any holding tank, purgatory or anything else. I will be going straight into His presence.

There are over six billion people on planet earth now, and in the time that it has taken you to read this there have probably been many hundreds who have let go of their earthly bodies in order to enjoy what you and I can only imagine now. They are present with Jesus. There are thousands upon thousands who have already made this passing ahead of us. Peter is there. Paul is there. Philip, Lazarus, John they are all there. You can think of many loved ones who are already there.

My mother, who has been a dear saint, has said to me many times, "I am not being morbid, but I am ready to go to be with the Lord. I have many more people there than I have here now." She said, "When you get the call and you come to my casket, don't be sad; I won't be and I don't want you to be." If I thought that my mother and my brothers and sisters were really going out to the graveyard in a box, I would not be able to cope. What I know is that all the boxes that I have carried to the grave are just bodies, just the earthly remains of those who have gone on to be with the Lord.

My friend who died in her twenties has been in the presence of the Lord for many years now. You could go out to her grave and see the marker, but she is not there. She has never been out there. We just carried her "tent" that had folded up out there. One day even that body is going to be raised up, immortal in glory!

So I don't want you to fear death. Jesus has defeated the Devil who had the power of death and He now has the keys to death. There is no fear for us because, "Precious in His sight is the death of his saints" (Psalm 116:15). When you finally let go of the earthly "tent" of your body you will be welcomed into the presence of the One who gave His life to set you free.

Prayer

Father, we thank you for your truth that sets us free from the fear of death. We thank you for the comfort that comes from knowing that if we are in Christ we really should have no fear of death. I pray that everyone who is reading these words will come to know Christ as Savior so that they too can be free. We thank you for all your truth. We know that if you Son Jesus sets us free, we are free indeed. By the power of your Spirit, help us to live out these truths so that we can know your more deeply and give others a taste of Your goodness. In Christ's Name, Amen.

Made in the USA
Columbia, SC
19 December 2021

52177078R00109